365 Ways to Prepare for Christmas

DAVID E. MONN
WITH
MARILYN J. APPLEBERG

 HarperCollins*Publishers*

A John Boswell Associates Book

HarperCollins books may be purchased for educational, business, or sales promotional use. For information, please write: Special Markets Department, HarperCollins Publishers, Inc., 10 East 53rd Street, New York, NY 10022.

FIRST EDITION

Design: Barbara Cohen Aronica
Illustrations: Jennifer Harper
Index: Maro Riofrancos

LIBRARY OF CONGRESS CATALOGING-IN-PUBLICATION DATA
Monn, David.
    365 ways to prepare for Christmas / David Monn.
        p.   cm.
    Includes index.
    ISBN 0-06-017048-4
    1. Christmas cookery.   2. Christmas.   3. Christmas decorations.
I. Title.   II. Title: Three hundred and sixty-five ways to prepare for Christmas.
TX739.2C45M66   1993
641.5'68—dc20   92-56214

93   94   95   96   97   HC   10   9   8   7   6   5   4   3   2   1

Dear Reader:

We welcome your recommendations for future 365 Ways books. Send your suggestions and a recipe, if you'd like, to Cookbook Editor, HarperCollins Publishers, 10 East 53rd Street, New York, NY 10022. If we choose your title suggestion or your recipe we will acknowledge you in the book and send you a free copy.

Thank you for your support.

Sincerely yours,
The Editor

CONTENTS

1   Avoiding the Trenches   3

Commonsense tips for avoiding the crush in December, including mail order from the top 22 specialty catalogs and a month-by-month calendar of what's on sale, and when, throughout the year.

2   Gather Ye Rosebuds . . . Hydrangeas, Baby's Breath, and Lavender, Too   10

It's amazing how many creative and enjoyable things there are to do year-round in anticipation of Christmas, from drying spring and summer flowers for holiday bouquets, collecting Christmas materials from Valentine's Day through the Fourth of July, Halloween, and Thanksgiving, to combing flea markets for vintage gifts, greeting cards, and toys. Also included here are recipes for gift giving anytime of year, such as flavored vinegars and other condiments.

3   Gift Buying: Getting It Right   27

Practical strategies and imaginative suggestions for what to give to those who have everything to those who have little, and everyone in between, including the family dog.

Handmade gifts and cards are ways of giving a part of yourself to those you care about. Here are ideas for simple one-of-a-kind cards, gifts from the heart, like the Family Tree and a Button Bracelet, and memorable edibles, like a Chocolate Applesauce Cake and Rum and Maple Cream Liqueur.

Wrapping gifts can be as much of a pleasure as making and buying them. And creating your own wraps presents extra opportunities for the family to share time during the busy holiday season. Even the kids can make Leaf Wrap and Vegetable Prints wrapping papers. Using recyclables like maps makes good ecological sense, and a recyclable wrap like the Incredible Edible Box tastes good too. Take a tip from It's in the Bag to turn even the lowly brown paper bag into something glamorous.

Here you'll find a multitude of quick and easy suggestions for holiday decorating. It's amazing what, for instance, nature's bounty and a little Christmas gilt can do for each other. Centerpieces, party favors, and ways to make use of Christmas scents are also included here.

The tree is the centerpiece of most holiday decors. Here are dozens of suggestions for easy ornaments to make, like *Patchwork Balls, Nostalgic Nosegays,* and *Paper Snowflakes.* Ideas are offered for thematic trees, such as the *Country Western Tree,* the *Americana Tree,* and the *Victorian Tree,* and alternative trees— tabletop trees, *Baby's First Tree,* and the *Love & Kisses Tree*—living trees, and even "untrees," such as the *Ladder Tree.*

Tips to make you look good because your Christmas fare tastes so good. Recipes are included here for such prepare-ahead dishes as *Mushrooms Stuffed with Crab* and *Cheesebread Soufflé,* as well as "instant classics," like the *Almond Christmas Wreath Bread.*

Complete menus with recipes for exciting holiday entertaining, from the Holiday Cocktail Party with *Wassail* and *Brioche Basket Filled with Brie* to a Christmas Eve Open House featuring *Wild Mushroom Lasagne* and a spectacular *Croquembouche.* The Irish Hunt Breakfast starts with non-alcoholic *Citrus Fizz* and ends with *Poached Pears with Irish Whiskey Sauce.* On Christmas Day, the Children's Christmas Table features *Crown Roast of Frankfurters with Baked Beans* and ends with *Almond Butter Cookies.* The sumptuous Victorian Christmas Dinner stars *Roast Goose with Sage and Onion Stuffing,* and the Traditional Christmas Dinner has as its centerpiece *Roast Turkey with Chicken Sausage Stuffing* and a glorious *Bûche de Noël* for dessert. *Bubble and*

Squeak is the main course of a Boxing Day Supper on December 26 and the Twelfth Night Dessert Party tempts with a *Champagne Punch Bowl* and *Amaretto Mousse.*

Desserts like *Eggnog Crème Brûlée, Lemon Poppyseed Cookies, Nutty Thumbprint* cookies, and even *Sugarplums* will dance out of your kitchen.

Christmas as we know it, from the aroma of a *Gingerbread Cottage* in the works to the mistletoe in the *Kissing Ball* you make. Create some new traditions as well by making a *Time Capsule,* sharing a quiet time reading aloud Dickens's *A Christmas Carol,* or arranging a progressive dinner.

Make a record of Christmas past and think about next year. We help by giving you space to list cards, gifts, parties, menus, and guests, and special notations you might want to make about ideas 1–360.

Introduction

Christmas is a time of year when cheer and goodwill abound and all things seem possible, even having dreams come true. Perhaps because it brings out the child in all of us, we once again seem capable of creativity, imagination, and the joyful, courageous abandon of our early years. We want to indulge our senses with sights, sounds, and aromas. Yet for many there is a down side to the holiday that comes from trying to do too much in too little time.

This book holds the key for a well-planned and most enjoyable holiday season. Every aspect of the season's delights is covered, from early preparations for Christmas to family activities, from quick and easy yet stylish holiday decorating to palate-pleasing recipes and complete yuletide menus for memorable entertaining. May you find here, in these pages, the secret to having a truly Merry Christmas!

PART ONE

It's Never Too Early

CHAPTER 1

Avoiding the Trenches

For those who want to avoid the anxiety and crush of last minute Christmas gift buying and the tradeoff between time and money—the later it is, the likelier you are to spend more— now is the time to begin getting ready for next Christmas. If need be, start with a New Year's resolution to never again find yourself wishing the holidays were over before they even begin. This chapter, indeed this entire book, is a game plan for how to have not only a sane Christmas but a highly enjoyable one. An integral part of the strategy is to avoid the trenches in December. Let's face it, nothing undermines those feelings of universal goodwill more than being elbowed in the ribs and feeling the urge to elbow back.

BASIC TRAINING

1   Create a Christmas Corner

Can anything be more frustrating than trying to remember where you put those gifts you bought early? Designate an area, be it a closet, cupboard, or just a carton or shopping bag to store all the gifts, tissue, paper, fabric, ribbons, dried flowers, and so on until you need them. You'll be surprised how far ahead of the game you are when you check them out in November.

2   Listing toward Christmas

There are people in your life who remain at the top of your gift list year after year. These are the people for whom it is easiest to buy ahead. Each has interests, hobbies, passions. You owe it to yourself to keep a list of these people handy, with their interests (sports, travel, gardening, etc.), their collections (handmade fishing flies, flamingos, advertising art, art deco jewelry, etc.), as well as their clothing sizes and color preferences noted.

3 ॐ Order of the Day

Mail-order catalogs present opportunities to shop without leaving your house (though some would consider this no fun at all), and sales on special items throughout the year offer the best for less.

Mail-order gifts may be bought at any time during the year, often at sale price. When ordering from a catalog, keep in mind that there is usually a shipping charge and that each company has its own return policy. Always have the gift sent to you so you can inspect the quality and condition and personalize the gift with a card. Here is a list of the best catalogs in several categories; just settle into your armchair and start shopping.

The Body Shop
45 Horsehill Road, Cedar Knolls, NJ 07927-2014. (800) 541-2535. British-based manufacturer and retailer of skin and hair care products. All are naturally based with no testing on animals. Ecologically and globally conscious; involved in rights of indigenous peoples.

Booksellers By Mail
2515 East 43rd Street, P.O. Box 182267, Chattanooga, TN 37422-7267. (800) 874-0524. Devoted to the best books in print. Over 400 books in 24 categories plus audio books and videos.

Chambers
P.O. Box 7841, San Francisco, CA 94120-7841. (800) 334-9790. Wonderful furnishings for bed and bath: Linens, towels, aromatic lotions, and luxurious bath accessories.

Childcraft, Inc.
P.O. Box 29149, Mission, KS 66201-9149. (800) 631-5657. Well-regarded source for toys and hobby kits for children of all ages.

Critics' Choice Video
P.O. Box 749, Itasca, IL 60143-0749. (800) 367-7765. Over 42,000 films available.

Exposures
2800 Hoover Road, Stevens Point, WI 54481. (800) 222-4947. Stylish picture frames and photo albums, including those with acid-free pages. Also decorative accessories, including display shelves, lamps, and more.

Hammacher Schlemmer
P.O. Box 182256, Chattanooga, TN 37422-7256. (800) 233-4800. The longtime source for every gadget you might conceivably need or want for home, office, airplane, or boat.

Hold Everything
P.O. Box 7807, San Francisco, CA 94120-7807. (800) 421-2264. Products to organize your home and simplify your life.

Horchow Home Collection
P.O. Box 620048, Dallas, TX 75262-0048. (800) 456-7000. Top-of-the-line home furnishings and accessories. Extended payment plan.

The Metropolitan Museum of Art
Box 255, Gracie Station, New York, NY 10028-9998. (800) 468-7386. Quality reproductions of antiquities and jewelry, as well as posters, books, scarves, and other stylish gifts.

Neiman-Marcus
P.O. Box 2968, Dallas, TX 75221-2968. (800) 825-8000. Texas-based retailer of note. Elegant women's fashions and accessories.

Orvis
1711 Blue Hills Drive, P.O. Box 1200, Roanoke, VA 24022-8001. (800) 541-3541. The nation's oldest mail-order company. Specialists with catalogs for fishermen and hunters, as well as travel, clothing for men and women, and gifts.

Pottery Barn
P.O. Box 7044, San Francisco, CA 94120-7044. (800) 922-5507. Well-designed accessories for the home; exceptional value.

Smith & Hawken
25 Corte Madera, Mill Valley, CA 94941. (415) 383-2000. Fax (415) 383-7030. Garden needs, including bulbs; also clothing, tools, holiday gifts, and furniture.

Starbucks Coffee Company
2203 Airport Way South, P.O. Box 34510, Seattle, WA 98124-1510. (800) 445-3428 (Monday–Saturday only). The finest coffees from around the globe. Also coffee accessories, including espresso machines and grinders. Works in partnership with CARE to fund children's health programs in Guatemala and Indonesia and literacy programs in Kenya.

Tiffany & Co.
801 Jefferson Road, P.O. Box 5477, Parsippany, NJ 07054-9957. (800) 526-0649. The prestigious treasure house has a wide range of gifts besides expensive jewelry, like playing cards, scarves, stationery, affordable silver pens, key chains, and bookmarks.

Van Bourgondien
245 Farmingdale Road, P.O. Box 1000, Babylon, NY 11702. (800) 622-9997. Quality Dutch and domestic bulbs and plants.

Victoria's Secret
P.O. Box 16589, Columbus, OH 43216-6589. (800) 888-8200. Feminine and sexy intimate apparel and sleepwear.

Wayside Gardens
1 Garden Lane, Hodges, SC 29695-0001. (800) 845-1124. Longtime well-regarded source for shrubs, plants, vegetables.

Williams-Sonoma
P.O. Box 7456, San Francisco, CA 94120-7456. (800) 541-2233. A name synonymous with fine cookware. Also offers serving pieces, table linens, recipe books, and some food ingredients.

Winterthur Museum and Gardens
Dover, DE 19901. (800) 767-0500. A collection of rare plants and unusual gifts from the famed museum.

Wireless
Minnesota Public Radio, P.O. Box 64422, St. Paul, MN 55164-0422. (800) 669-9999. Nostalgic audio selections including vintage radio programs, as well as videos, witty T-shirts, and other gifts.

4 ⚑ To Every Month There Is a Sale

Shopping for Christmas gifts throughout the year is a strategy that works, just ask anyone who does it. Following is a calendar of the type of sales held in department and specialty stores throughout the year; bold type indicates choice Christmas gift-shopping opportunities.

* *January:* **Continuation of after-Christmas sales; lingerie; accessories; luggage; stationery; white sales;** winter clearance of shoes, boots, clothing, **furs, ski clothing and gear; knitting, needlework, and craft supplies; toiletries, fragrances, cosmetics, and beauty treatments;** semiannual furniture sale.
* *February:* Lincoln's, Washington's, and Presidents' Day storewide sales; housewares; fabric; electronics; hosiery. Preseason sales of barbecue grills, outdoor furniture, lawn mowers.
* *March:* Spring sales storewide; **china and glassware crystal accessories, silver and stainless flatware;** floor coverings; do-it-yourself home improvement equipment; pre-Easter fashions.
* *April:* Starting Easter Sunday: outdoor furniture, garden supplies, summer table accessories, and rugs. After-Easter clearance (in March if Easter occurs then); **sleepwear, at-home wear;** yard goods, trimmings, patterns for summer fashions; **diamond and gold jewelry; watches.**
* *May:* **White sales; baby needs;** gifts for brides and graduates; summer housewares including picnic gear, home furnishings; luggage; **pre–Mother's Day sales of jewelry, small accessories, scarves;** Memorial Day sales: summer fashions, sporting equipment, outdoor furniture and gear.

- *June:* Summer appliances; **golf, tennis, fishing, and camping equipment; sport shoes and clothing;** swimsuits; luggage; floor coverings; for Father's Day, **men's furnishings, accessories, games, small leather goods.**
- *July:* Storewide Fourth of July sales in every category of merchandise, especially summer swimwear and fashions; semiannual furniture sale; **furs.**
- *August:* Final summer clearance sales; early fall accessories; stationery and school supplies; **toys;** continuation of fur and semiannual furniture sales, pre–Labor Day sales of back-to-school wear.
- *September:* Labor Day sales storewide on fall and some winter fashions; **school equipment sales,** computers, calculators, briefcases; **major housewares sale of the year: cutlery, gadgets, tools, gifts, casual china and glass, small and large appliances;** do-it-yourself home equipment tools, hardware, paint, and wallpaper; **home entertainment equipment.**
- *October:* Columbus Day sale of outerwear, fall fashions, home furnishings, floor covering; **infant needs;** preseason ski sales.
- *November:* Election Day and Veterans Day, the two major prewinter sales of outerwear for the whole family; fall and winter fashions, and accessories; curtain and drapery sales; lamps; pre-Thanksgiving sale of **china, glass, tablecloths, silverware, pots, pans, serving pieces, small appliances; post-Thanksgiving sale (in reality the start of the Christmas shopping season); furs, skates, skis, sleds, bikes.**
- *December:* **Holiday fashions; infant and toddler clothes and gifts; gourmet foods; after-Christmas sales: half-price Christmas cards, tree trimmings, gift wrap, toys, holiday candy, cakes, and cookies; giftware and small home furnishings items.**

CHAPTER 2

Gather Ye Rosebuds . . . Hydrangeas, Baby's Breath, and Lavender, Too

With a little forethought and without a lot of work, much can be done throughout the year to ensure a creative Christmas holiday season. Most of the efforts are doubly rewarding, for many handmade presents, cards, invites, and decorations are also ecologically sound. Recycling makes sense for your family and for the family of man.

5 ❦ Making Preservations

During the spring, summer, and fall, whenever you pick wild-flowers, or buy a bouquet of flowers, or are given roses, think ahead to Christmas. Dried flowers make splendid additions to packages, wreaths, garlands, and topiary. They represent one of the easiest and nicest ways to recycle Mother Nature's bounty. Always work with flowers and herbs when they are fresh and dry (not wet from rain or dew).

6 ❦ Drying Flowers

Such flowers as sweetheart roses, hydrangeas, yarrow, baby's breath, heather, statice, and larkspur may be air-dried simply by hanging them in bunches upside down, where air can circulate around them. More fragile flowers and those with many petals may be preserved with silica, which absorbs the moisture while preserving the shape of the flower. Gently insert a piece of florist wire into the flower so it will stand. Fill a jar halfway with silica crystals. Place the flower upright in the middle of the jar and gently pour in enough crystals to go in between and to cover all the petals. Seal the container for at least two weeks, then remove the flower. The silica crystals may be reused.

7 ❦ Drying Herbs

Several fragrant herbs are associated with Christmas: English pennyroyal, lavender, wild thyme, and rosemary. The first three are identified with the Christ Child; the last is said to bring happiness to those who smell it on Christmas Eve. Dried herbs retain their fragrance for use in potpourri, wreaths, and tree decorations, not to mention cooking. They are found at farmers' markets, some supermarkets, and gourmet shops, or perhaps, in your own garden.

To dry fresh herbs, gather the sprigs into small bunches, tie each tightly with string, and hang upside down from a nail or hanger in a place where air will circulate around them. Allow the herbs to dry for about ten days. If not used soon after drying, gently wrap the herbs in tissue paper, and store where they won't be crushed.

8 Holiday Gathering

There are several holidays during the year when you can buy raw materials to use for Christmas. The best of the genre is available then.

- Valentine's Day: The heart is a timeless folk art symbol that is used generously in decorating for Christmas. Valentine's Day is the time to find paper hearts, foil hearts, wooden hearts, satin hearts; heart stickers; heart mobiles; heart quilts; heart-shaped candy boxes and doilies; and antique and reproduction Valentine cards with illustrations useful for decoupage gifts, handmade ornaments, and gift wrapping. Also see the Love & Kisses Tree, page 124.
- Easter: This is the season for small inexpensive wicker baskets with handles and plastic eggs to use to make Christmas decorations and ornaments (see page 128).
- Fourth of July: For nineteenth-century Americans, the flag was a major motif on Christmas trees, not just for Independence Day and other patriotic occasions. Take a decorating cue from their book and on the Fourth of July collect as many as you can of the following:

  • Miniature paper flags of the kind used in drinks and hors d'oeuvres (available in packages at party paper stores); they add interest to ornaments such as Santas and snowmen.

  • Paper plates decorated with small flags or red, white, and blue stripes to make ornaments.

  • Small cloth flags, given out or sold by veterans organizations to wave at parades (contact your local VFW to see about purchasing in bulk), to tuck into an exuberantly decorated Americana tree.

  • American flag fans, available in novelty and card shops to place in a tree trimmed in the style of the nineteenth century.
- Halloween: Buy packages of wrapped miniature candies to

make a wreath (see page 90) and fill cornucopias (see page 130); for the best price wait until the day after Halloween. Be sure to hide away these goodies until they are needed for Christmas. Recycle the miniature pumpkins and gourds you used to decorate for Halloween as Christmas decorations by gilding them with gold paint.

• Thanksgiving: Lavish centerpieces of fresh fruit are often left over after the Thanksgiving feast. Gild some of the leftover apples, oranges, pineapples, star fruit, and grapes to use in wreaths, topiaries, tabletop and mantelpiece decoration.

9 ᛝ Vacations throughout the Year

No matter where in the world you go for your vacation there are ample opportunities to shop, so be sure to have your Christmas gift list with you—even if you are vacationing in February.

• Buy inexpensive, colorful souvenirs, handmade, if possible, and from that place. They make unusual decorations and your tree will become a reminder of where you have been. Among the items to consider are snow shaker globes, dolls, fans, and key chains.

• Collect seashells on an island or shore vacation for use as tree trimmings, to wrap presents, or as table adornments.

• Visit museums and even if you don't spend much time viewing the collections, check out the gift shop for books and unusual postcards to use as invites, as Christmas cards, or as tree trimmings. Look for classic gifts among the reproductions of antiquities and jewelry.

• Save ticket and admission stubs, picture postcards, small denominations of money and stamps (if foreign travel), labels from wine bottles, plane, train, and ship tickets, luggage tags, road and street maps to be combined with snapshots to make a memory box (see page 54) or a collage (see page 53) as a gift for your travel companion. Many of these bits and pieces can also go into the design for a decoupage box (see page 55).

10 🎄 Fair Market Value

Spring through fall, street fairs, flea markets, and indoor and outdoor antique shows present an unequaled opportunity for Christmas shopping. Even if you yourself are not a collector, these markets are a source of inexpensive gifts (have your list with you) as well as unique and relatively inexpensive raw materials for making your own gifts, cards, wraps, and ornaments.

11 🎄 Old Lace

Much of the lace found at flea markets is handmade and more detailed and delicate than its modern counterpart. Add lace collars to storebought sweaters; use odd pieces of lace fabric, trim, and ribbon for handmade ornaments, cards, Christmas stockings, wraps, and gifts. Also see the Victorian Tree, page 136.

12 🎄 Buttons & Buckles

Boxes and jars of buttons are an inexpensive source of inspiration. Older buttons and buckles are often unusually shaped; many are made of ivory, Bakelite, cut steel, mother-of-pearl, or glass; some are hand-painted, filigreed, or fabric covered. Use them as trimming on a vest or T-shirt or for decorating a plain inexpensive picture frame. Make a button bracelet and earrings, button covers, a brooch, gift ribbons, and a Christmas ornament.

13 🎄 Making Book

Old books, including nineteenth-century editions, can cost as little as two dollars. Don't overlook those in poor condition, as they can be a source of prints that when framed (even inexpensively) make lovely gifts. Old nursery rhyme books are ubiquitous and the charming illustrations, framed, are perfect for a child's room.

14 ❧ Seasoned Greetings

German immigrant Louis Prang is known as the "father of the American Christmas card," and the artistic cards turned out by his studio in the 1870s and 1880s are true collector's items. His larger cards, in accordance with popular Victorian taste, were bordered with silk fringe. If you find a Prang, treasure it, but Christmas cards from the 1920s, 1930s, and 1940s are just as interesting to the noncollector for use as nostalgic tree trimmings. Glue small Victorian ones to a lace doily and hang with a hook or ribbon.

15 ❧ Toys Were Us

Vintage toys evoke memories of a simpler time and lend an old-fashioned magic to today's Christmas decorating. Old teddy bears, wooden toy soldiers, rag dolls, wooden blocks, mechanical toys, pre-Barbie dolls, folk toys, tops, and sleds are instant heirlooms. Create nostalgic vignettes in any room of the house or use as decoration near or under the tree.

16 ❧ Hat Tricks

Old-fashioned handmade milliner's trimmings, such as velvet and silk flowers, bunches of cherries, and exotic feathers, are pretty additions to a gift basket or to a handmade card, or as tree ornaments.

17 ❧ Mirror, Mirror

Small or oddly shaped old mirrors with interesting frames are usually inexpensive and once you give them the Cinderella treatment they make memorable gifts. Mirrors add to the glow in decorating for the holidays, so keep one or two for yourself.

18 🎄 Cookie Cutters & Candy Molds

Vintage cookie cutters are fun to collect, both for Christmas baking and as ornaments and gifts (see pages 17 and 126). Antique candy molds that feature multiples of Santa, reindeer, hearts, trees, and other Christmas images have special appeal as holiday decorative objects.

19 🎄 Patch It Up

Not every patchwork quilt started was finished. Large and small colorful unassembled quilt pieces pop up regularly at flea markets, often in batches, and they add a pretty touch to packages, handmade ornaments (see page 128), and Christmas stockings (see page 113).

20 🎄 Tie One On

The rich dark hues of vintage men's silk ties lend themselves to handmade sachets (see page 107) to give as gifts or to hang on your tree.

21 🎄 Singles Wanted

A single sterling napkin ring, bone china cup and saucer, dessertspoon, or silver serving piece often are among the mismatched pieces found at flea markets. Each makes a unique gift on its own or creatively combined with something else (see page 33). Your gift may also mark the beginning of a highly personal collection to which you can add each Christmas.

22 🎄 All That Glitters

Most sellers of old costume jewelry have loose bits and pieces of trinkets, including unstrung pearls, crystals, and rhinestones, all of which make festive elements for handmade cards (see page 45) and tree ornaments (see page 135).

23 🎄 Jarring

Pretty or interestingly shaped jars and bottles make those home-made gifts of sauces, vinegars, liqueurs, and mustards from your kitchen even more special. A kitschy vintage cookie jar helps the memory of a delectable edible gift last that much longer.

24 🎄 Pass the Salt

Antique crystal or pressed-glass saltshakers, though missing their silver-plated tops, make dainty bud vases to place at each setting on your holiday table. Look for old inkwells without lids for the same purpose.

25 🎄 Ornamental Charm

Many dealers of country items feature turn–of–the–century blown-glass tree ornaments year round. Prices have climbed in recent years, but for purists their beauty is unmatched by modern reproductions. One of these unique decorations is a lovely lasting present to be used and cherished every year.

26 🎄 The Real Thing

Antique and flea markets and street fairs are treasure troves of such one-of-a-kind Christmas presents as vintage kitchen utensils, stoneware crocks, handpainted ceramic bowls, pitchers, and platters; silver, mosaic, or enameled picture frames; baskets; writing implements; antique table and bed linens; and lace. In most instances you pay less for an original than for a modern reinterpretation of lesser quality. Remember when buying at these markets that there are usually no returns. Check the merchandise carefully; the dealers expect you to do so.

NATURE GIFTS

As part of your program to get a head start on Christmas, make Mother Nature your partner in creating gifts.

27 ⟨N⟩ Forced Beauty

Pots of ready-to-bloom bulbs make thoughtful Christmas presents and are an easy and inexpensive way to fill a house with fresh flowers for the holidays. Of course, you can buy them in a florist shop, but this is a great rainy day project in which to involve the whole family, including young children. Bulbs are forced or coaxed into bloom by using water, light, and temperature to fool the bulb into thinking spring has arrived. You need just a handful of bulbs, which you can buy at a nursery or from a gardening catalog, a flower pot or other container, some potting soil or gravel, and water. When you are ready to present your gifts of flowering plants, cover the soil with sheet moss and a few pinecones. To make the presentation more festive, tie a two-inch-wide wire-edged ribbon in muted earth tones around the rim of the pot. The two easiest bulbs to force are paperwhite narcissus and amaryllis.

28 ⟨N⟩ Paperwhites: Six Weeks to Bloom

These are best forced in a shallow pot or bowl *without* drainage holes in the bottom. Fill the pot two-thirds full with gravel. Place the paperwhite bulbs (as many as will fit in the container) on the gravel, pointed end up, then fill in gravel around them. The more bulbs you use in one container the more spectacular the display. Fill the pot with water until it reaches the bottom of the bulbs. Set the container in a dark cool (45° to 50°F) spot. When roots have developed—about three weeks—move the pot to a sunny cool spot. Shoots will develop rapidly and in about three more weeks you'll have masses of fragrant delicate white flowers, which will last for up to ten days. Present the plants just as they are ready to blossom.

29 ⚘ Amaryllis: Six to Eight Weeks to Bloom

Amaryllis requires a much larger pot to hold just one bulb. Choose an aged clay pot (see below) with drainage hole and a saucer. Before potting, soak the bulb overnight in lukewarm water. Spread a shallow layer of gravel, pot shards, or other drainage materials in the bottom of the pot. Add several inches of soil and place the bulb in the pot with the pointed end of the bulb just peeking above the rim of the pot. Add more soil and gently pat it down around the bulb, leaving the top exposed. Water until the soil is moist but not soaked. Place the pot in a sunny cool spot. Water sparingly for a few weeks, until the appearance of the first shoot, then water more often, so that the soil is always moist. In about six to eight weeks you have a tall exotic-looking plant with a cluster of huge red, pink, peach, orange, or multicolored flowers. Time your potting so your gift will be ready to present just before the buds open.

30 ⚘ Going to Pot?

A plan-ahead step to take during the summer is the aging or weathering of clay pots to use for gifts of seasonal bulbs as well as topiaries (see page 98). Turn new clay pots upside down and rub buttermilk all over them. Leave them for three weeks in a shaded, damp, area, such as a damp, dark basement or garage. If you live in an apartment, you can create the right environment by placing the pots in a cardboard box covered with a large plastic bag.

31 🔥 Think before You Toss

During the year gather the following to put in your Christmas corner: wide-mouth jars and narrow-neck bottles (jelly glasses, salad dressing bottles, glass soda bottles) to store and give gifts from the kitchen; brown paper grocery, lunch, and shopping bags and plain brown wrapping paper from mailings to make gift wraps; white paper bakery bags to make luminaries; mailing tubes, paper towel and toilet tissue rolls to make gift wraps and party favors; the tops of frozen juice containers, the cardboard from new shirts, and the backing of legal- and letter-size yellow pads to make ornaments; wine and champagne corks to make stamps.

32 🔥 When to Mail

Buy stamps, packing boxes, and brown shipping paper before Thanksgiving or during the first week in December. Get your domestic cards and gift packages into the mail no later than two weeks before Christmas. If you are mailing overseas (first class), allow at least three weeks; for non-first-class mail, you had best allow six weeks for delivery. Send out holiday party invites during the first week in December, when people are marking their calendars with upcoming events (you should be doing the same). An added benefit to mailing early is avoiding those long lines at the post office.

33 🔥 How to Pack for Mailing

When you need to pad a package, recycle wherever possible. Instead of bubblewrap and Styrofoam use newspaper. If someone you know has a paper shredder, ask for a bagful of the results; you can also use the edges of computer paper. Use stale air-popped popcorn (not buttered) and include a note instructing the recipients to keep the gift and give the birds the popcorn.

GIFTS FROM THE KITCHEN

Vinegars and condiments are among the gifts from your kitchen that may be prepared at least a month before Christmas. For more gifts from the kitchen see pages 57–66.

34 🎵 Garlic Herb Vinegar

PREP: 10 minutes   COOK: none   STAND: 1 month
MAKES: 1 quart

When combined with extra-virgin olive oil, this infused vinegar transforms ordinary lettuce into a three-star salad. Package in a pretty cork-topped bottle tied at the neck with a red and white checked table napkin.

1 cup (packed) fresh basil sprigs,   *8 garlic cloves*
   or other herbs, such as thyme,   *4 cups red wine vinegar, plus*
   rosemary, or tarragon   *more, if necessary*

    1. Rinse basil and dry thoroughly between towels. Divide between 2 sterile pint jars. Crush garlic cloves with side of a knife, discarding papery skin. Add 4 garlic cloves to each jar. Pour in vinegar and cap jars tightly.

    2. Let jars stand in a sunny window, turning every few days, for 1 month. Check periodically to be sure herbs are covered with vinegar; add fresh vinegar as necessary. The vinegar can be stored at room temperature up to 4 months.

35 ﴾ Raspberry Vinegar

PREP: 10 minutes   COOK: 3 to 5 minutes   STAND: 2 weeks
MAKES: 1 quart

If you plan ahead and purchase raspberries in season at your local farmers' market, making this luxurious vinegar can be quite economical. Present the pint jars in a small wicker basket lined with a colorful cotton dish towel and tied with raffia.

6 cups raspberries   *16 perfect raspberries*
4 cups unseasoned rice wine
   vinegar or white wine vinegar

1. Sort through berries, discarding stems or any that are moldy. Set aside 16 of the most perfect berries.

2. Place 3 cups berries in each of 2 sterile heatproof quart jars. In a medium nonreactive saucepan, gently warm vinegar over low heat until just heated through, 3 to 5 minutes. Pour warm vinegar over berries, dividing evenly, and cap tightly. Let mixture stand 2 weeks, shaking daily.

3. Pour mixture through a cheesecloth–lined sieve set over a bowl, pressing down on berries to extract as much juice as possible. Discard berry seeds and pulp.

4. Place 8 raspberries in each of 2 sterile pint jars, cover with vinegar, and cap tightly. Raspberry vinegar can be stored at room temperature up to 1 year.

36 🌢 Tarragon Mustard

PREP: 10 minutes   COOK: none   MAKES: about 2¼ cups

Whether slathered on sandwiches or served as an accompaniment to pork or poultry, this fragrant mustard is always a favorite. Present in an old glass jelly jar (stripped of labels) and add a small wooden spoon to a bright bow tied around the top.

2 cups Dijon mustard
2 tablespoons minced fresh tar-
    ragon, or 2 teaspoons dried,
    crumbled

1 tablespoon extra-virgin olive oil
2 teaspoons white wine vinegar
Dash of cayenne

In a medium bowl, combine mustard, tarragon, olive oil, vinegar, and cayenne. Whisk to blend well. Refrigerate in a tightly covered container up to 1 month.

37 🌢 Spiced Honey Mustard

PREP: 5 minutes   COOK: none   MAKES: about 2½ cups

This versatile mustard is particularly good with ham or grilled sausages and makes an easy-to-prepare gift for a hostess. Pack in a glass or ceramic jar pretty enough to keep on the dinner table.

2 cups Dijon mustard
1/2 cup honey

1/2 teaspoon ground cumin
1/4 teaspoon ground allspice

In a small bowl, combine mustard, honey, cumin, and allspice. Whisk to blend well. Refrigerate in a tightly covered container up to 1 month.

PART TWO

Gifts, Cards, Wraps, & Invites

CHAPTER 3

Gift Buying:
Getting It Right

No aspect of the holiday experience is more
fraught with anxiety than the desire to get the
gift giving right. It brings into play judgment,
taste, and creativity, as well as finance; no
wonder it's so unnerving. If you follow the
advice in Chapter 1, you'll eliminate much
of that apprehension by implementing a few
simple think- and plan-ahead strategies.
This chapter focuses on the art of gift giving.
Whether choosing to spend less or to spend
more, to buy a single gift or to combine
presents, to give of oneself, or to contribute
money, finding the appropriate gift is most
assuredly an art.

38 🕯 Shopping Tactics

- Try to shop in the early morning, before the salespeople have become overwhelmed and stocks depleted; you'll be less tired then too.
- Go shopping with your list in hand or at least a game plan; this is no time to let inspiration be your guide.
- Think of alternatives to department stores, places where you won't encounter the Christmas crush:

    Art-supply stores for stationery items, such as handmade papers, imported brushes to be used for makeup, fine writing instruments, attractive portfolios for storage.

    Stationers for many of the same items found in art-supply stores, plus leather memo books, calendars, and diaries.

    Museum gift shops for gifts of art reproductions, skillfully crafted jewelry, educational books and toys, art books.

    Hardware stores for gadgets and widgets.
- Instead of buying several small gifts for each member of a family, buy a family present, such as a hammock for the back-yard or patio, a Ping-Pong set for the playroom, challenging computer software, or a video or CD sampler.
- People close to you often let you know indirectly what they want. Pay attention to hints, listen, and remember. Better yet, write it down on your list.
- Give yourself the gift of a bill-free January. Whenever possible pay cash for Christmas presents; it's also one way to ensure you won't go too far over budget.
- Before Thanksgiving, stock up on stamps, batteries, film, glasses, paper products, and any other staples you might need. If you intend to give gifts from the kitchen or entertain, this is also the time to pick up the nonperishables and beverages.
- If your gift list gets too long, agree with friends and family to give gifts only to the children. Many will feel relieved at this suggestion.

39 ❧ The Simple Things

Kids still get pleasure from simple things: a large box of crayons and a thick packet of construction paper; modeling clay; Play-Doh; pick-up sticks, a sack of colorful marbles, a Slinky, or a wooden jigsaw puzzle. Tinkertoys, Erector sets, and LEGO are all still popular ways to challenge a child's imagination. Dolls are a necessary ingredient of fantasy, and cuddly stuffed animals represent security and warmth; they're never out of style. Classics like Raggedy Ann and Andy, Paddington, and Babar are great to give with books about their adventures. For older children, familiar games like Scrabble and Monopoly or a chess set are good choices. And would Christmas be complete without an electric train set under the tree?

40 ❧ Repack It

Even if you don't cook or bake, you can still give food as gifts. Buy in quantity and personalize each gift by repacking it yourself in a reproduction or antique tin, vintage mason jar, new or old ceramicware. The container becomes part of the gift. Do this with fresh blends of coffee, ground loose or in the bean; tea; nuts; carob-covered raisins; seasonings; or dried fruit.

41 ❧ Catering

A foolproof way to giving the right gift is to cater to hobbies, pastimes, and avocations.

- *For the oenophile:* A bottle of fine wine or champagne.
- *For the tennis player or golfer:* Lessons with the pro.
- *For the theater buff:* Tickets to a hot show or a subscription to a local repertory theater.
- *For the cook, gardener, or craftsperson:* The latest book or video on their subject or a subscription to a newsletter (also see page 30).

- *For the ballet- or opera-lover:* Tickets to an upcoming event or membership in the guild.
- *For the football, baseball, hockey, or basketball fan:* Season tickets.
- *For the antiques or car-racing buff:* A subscription to the best magazine on the subject.
- *For the photographer or artist:* Supplies—no one ever has enough.
- *For the naturalist:* Membership to the local public television station.

42 ⚜ Lifestyle Gifts

- *For the stressed:* A shiatsu massage.
- *For a friend who prides him- or herself on a beautiful bedroom:* A set of designer sheets, a duvet cover, or antique pillow shams.
- *For the traveler:* A currency conversion calculator, electrical adaptor, language tapes, money belt, travel diary.
- *For the gourmand:* A food lover's newsletter or gift certificate to a fine restaurant.
- *For the busy executive:* An elegant planner, books on tape.
- *For the new parents:* A gift certificate for babysitting on demand.
- *For someone with a new business:* Accounting software.
- *For your older brother:* One sparkling car wash.

43 ⚜ For Someone Who Has Everything

- An evening on the town complete with chauffeur-driven Rolls-Royce.
- A case of the finest champagne, Bollinger.
- A dozen Baccarat champagne flutes.
- A seven-ounce tin of beluga caviar and a silver spoon for serving.
- A three-day trip to a warm tropical island on Presidents' Weekend.
- An in-town weekend at the city's best hotel.

- A shopping spree attended by a personal shopper in the best store in town.
- A day/weekend at a spa in or out of town.
- A ride in a hot-air balloon.
- The services of a personal trainer for six months.

44 ✍ Giving unto Others — The True Spirit of Christmas

- Help decorate the home and fill the refrigerator of an elderly neighbor.
- Deliver baskets of homemade Christmas goodies decorated with red and green balloons to hospital patients.
- Play Santa, complete with costume, to a children's hospital ward.
- Help organize a holiday party at a nursing home.
- Spend Christmas Eve working in a soup kitchen.
- Invite a family from a local shelter to have Christmas dinner with your family.
- Instead of giving presents one year, donate to a variety of charities in the name of each friend and family member; suggest they do the same as your gift.
- Organize a canned food drive at your church or local supermarket.
- Find out if your area police station or firehouse might be interested in starting a toy drive for needy children or a coat drive for the homeless.
- Donate your services as chauffeur to an otherwise homebound elderly person.
- Offer an evening or weekend of babysitting to someone who can't afford a babysitter.

45 ✿ Generic Gifts

One way to make things easy on yourself is to settle on a generic gift, one which is stylish yet suits several people on your list. Here are a few suggestions:

- A silver picture frame with a perpetual calendar is suitable for both men and women. The store can often personalize it with engraving at no extra charge.
- A sterling silver pen, also suitable for women and men, is not as expensive as you might think. For added panache order from Tiffany & Co.
- Reed & Barton, Spode, Lenox, and Wedgwood produce a splendid array of modestly priced sterling, silver-plated, crystal, and china Christmas ornaments and bells meant to be collected; each is engraved with the year.
- A handsome pocket-size leather-bound book for memos, notes about meals, wines, and birthday reminders can be embossed with the recipient's initials.
- A small but elegant crystal or handblown bud vase.

46 ✿ Stocking Stuffers

- Fragrant soap.
- Scented candle.
- Coffee mug.
- Folding umbrella.

- Packable tote bag.
- Walkman radio.
- Pocket calculator.
- Hair accessories.

47 ✿ Good-for-the-Earth Gifts

- Solar-powered calculator or watch.
- Low-flow showerhead or faucet aerator.
- String shopping bag.

- Reusable coffee filter.
- Natural deodorant crystal.
- Compost starter mix.
- Cedar cubes or hangers.

CREATIVE COMBINATIONS

Gifts like these take a little planning, but they always turn out to be greater than the sum of the parts.

48 ⟨▚ Tea for One

A thoughtful gift for the tea drinker on your list: An antique cup and saucer, easily found at a flea market, thrift shop, or garage sale—though it's not easy to find two or more that match. Before buying, run your hand along the rim of the cup and the edge of the saucer to check for chips. Fill the cup with English Breakfast, herbal, or decaffeinated fruit-flavored tea bags. Wrap in a piece of clear cellophane gathered at the top and tied with a lavish bow. This can be the start of a lovely tradition, with a gift of a different antique cup and saucer, and teas, each year.

49 ⟨▚ Not Your Cup of Tea?

For the coffee drinker: A French ceramic bowl, the perfect size for café au lait. Combine it with a bag of aromatic French Roast coffee and a reusable coffee filter.

50 ⟨▚ "Stirred Not Shaken"

For the martini-lover on your list who, like James Bond, is particular about how his martini is prepared: The makings of a perfect martini. A bottle each of gin and dry vermouth, a classic martini glass, a jar of olives, a copy of one of Ian Fleming's thrillers in either book or video form, and, of course, a cocktail stirrer.

51 ♠ "A Jug of Wine, A Loaf of Bread"

A romantic gift for someone with a literary bent: A wicker picnic hamper packed with a bottle of wine, a loaf of interesting bread, such as fig anise or olive, and a copy of Omar Khayyam's "The Rubaiyat."

52 ♠ Pasta Puttanesca Basket

For someone who likes Italian food: A basket or a bright enameled or wire colander filled with a box of imported pasta, a blend of Italian spices, a bottle of olive oil, and a recipe for Pasta Puttanesca. Tie the parsley to the handle with a raffia bow at the last minute. Here is a shopping list, followed by the recipe:

- Basket and cloth napkin
- Raffia or ribbon
- 1 pound spaghetti or rigatoni
- 1 small bottle extra-virgin olive oil
- 1 (15-ounce) can whole peeled tomatoes
- 1 (10-ounce) jar Kalamata olives
- 1 (4-ounce) jar capers
- 1 (2-ounce) can flat anchovy fillets
- 1 (1.4-ounce) jar crushed red pepper
- 1 bunch flat-leaf Italian parsley
- 1 head garlic

53 Pasta Puttanesca

PREP: 15 minutes   COOK: 8 to 10 minutes   SERVES: 4 to 6

This classic supposedly originated in the red-light district of Naples, as it could be quickly prepared between "engagements." Spaghetti is the traditional pasta choice, but some prefer a shape that captures more of the hot and spicy sauce with every bite.

1 pound spaghetti or hollow pasta with ridges, such as rigatoni
½ cup extra-virgin olive oil
3 large garlic cloves, crushed through a press
1 (2-ounce) can flat anchovy fillets, drained and coarsely chopped
1 (15-ounce) can whole peeled tomatoes, drained and coarsely chopped

¼ to ½ teaspoon crushed hot red pepper, to taste
¼ teaspoon freshly ground black pepper
⅛ teaspoon sugar
1 cup Kalamata olives, pitted and coarsely chopped
2 tablespoons drained capers
¼ cup chopped parsley

1. Cook pasta in a large pot of boiling salted water until tender but still firm, 8 to 10 minutes.

2. Meanwhile, in a large nonreactive frying pan, heat olive oil over medium heat. Stir in garlic and anchovies and cook until fragrant, about 1 minute. Add tomatoes, hot pepper, black pepper, and sugar. Cook, stirring occasionally, until sauce thickens slightly, 7 to 9 minutes.

3. Drain pasta and toss in a large warmed bowl with sauce, olives, capers, and parsley. Serve immediately.

54 Bathed in Luxury

For the sybarite on your list: A bath caddy, loofah, fragrant soaps, and a bath towel embroidered with the word "Mine." Pack it all into a flowered cardboard underbed box, which can be later used for storage.

55 ⟨ℕ⟩ Personal Property

Office supplies are always welcome: Yellow pads personalized with a rubber stamp, which becomes part of the gift; a few packs of Post-its in various sizes and colors; and colored paper clips. Pack it all in a wastepaper basket tied with a big crinkly paper bow.

56 ⟨ℕ⟩ New Year's Special

Give the ingredients of a special holiday toast: Two champagne flutes, a bottle of champagne and a stopper to keep it bubbly. For New Year's Eve, add packets of confetti and streamers. Pack it all in a painter's cardboard mixing bucket filled with loose confetti and shredded colored paper; wrap with Mylar gathered at the top and tied with a black bow tie.

57 ⟨ℕ⟩ Morning Glory

Offer the fixings for breakfast in bed: A wicker breakfast tray with a thermos carafe to keep the coffee hot; a down-filled neck roll; and a year's home delivery of the New York Times or Wall Street Journal.

58 ⟨ℕ⟩ Anticipate the Vernal Equinox

For the gardener: A terra-cotta planter that you have patinated (see page 19), filled with seed packets, bulbs for spring planting, gardening gloves, and a trowel.

59 ⟨ℕ⟩ Book Cover

Expand the gift of a cookbook with appropriate kitchen tools: A whisk and a wooden spoon with a dessert cookbook; a garlic roaster with a book of Mediterranean-style recipes; a vertical poultry roaster for a collection of chicken recipes.

60 ⁘ Sweet Treat

Fill an old cookie jar—whimsical, beautiful, or just plain functional—that you found at a flea market or collectibles shop with your own home-baked cookies. Write out the recipe on a card and attach it to the jar.

61 ⁘ Handy Person Special

For the apartment dweller: A toolbox filled with a hammer, screwdriver, wrench, tape, nails, and picture hooks.

62 ⁘ Gift Giving Caveats

- Don't surprise someone with a gift of a pet or you may find yourself with another mouth to feed.
- Know and respect a person's convictions before you buy things made of fur, ivory, or alligator or other so-called exotic skins.
- Don't give a gift that undermines someone's resolve about breaking a habit. No home-baked cookies, for instance, or cakes for someone on a diet, or a cigarette lighter for someone trying to quit smoking.
- Be careful with "self-improvement" gifts. No diet books or exercise tapes for the overweight or out-of-shape. Think twice about giving a beauty "makeover."

63 ॐ Not All Presents Are Tucked in a Stocking or Go under the Tree

- Delivery of fresh croissants and coffee from the local bakery every Saturday morning.
- Delivery of one perfect rose to the office every Monday morning for a year.
- A gift of long-distance calls for someone with family far away.
- A winter's worth of firewood for a city dweller with a fireplace.
- A gift certificate for spring delivery of a flowering plant or tree for the garden or roof terrace.

64 ॐ Holiday Tipping

Tipping may vary, depending on where you live and the level of service. In general holiday tipping is optional if you tip year-round.

- Housekeeper, nanny, au pair: One week's pay.
- Newspaper carrier: $5 to $10.
- Baby-sitter: The equivalent of two nights.
- Building superintendent: $25 to $50 ($75 in high-rent buildings).
- Doorman: $10 to $30.
- Garage attendant (monthly): $10 to $25.
- Hair stylist: A personal gift is more appropriate than money.

65 ॐ And Don't Forget to Remember

Make a basket of homemade cookies or other Christmas goodies for those you rely on throughout the year—the school-bus driver, crossing guard, bank teller or manager, nurse in your doctor's office, the men and women at the local firehouse and police precinct, the sanitation people. The gift need not be elaborate; the fact you remembered will be appreciated.

66 🐾 Pet Considerations

Most people who have pets consider them part of the family; they will be touched if you remember Fido or Kitty with a small gift. In general pets prefer food to toys; wrap biscuits or treats loosely in tissue paper and enjoy watching them unwrap the gift.

- A gift for both dog and master is a mason jar decorated with rubber-stamped paw prints and filled with dog biscuits. Include the rubber stamp as part of the gift.
- Give the Kitty of the house a catnip toy, and the owner will be pleased as well.

CHAPTER 4

When You Care Enough to Make the Very Best

Christmas gifts you make yourself always
include a "secret ingredient"—love.
Handmade Christmas cards and party invites
need not be elaborate to be memorable; they
just need to be personal.
Making your own Christmas gifts can be a
way of saving money, but the biggest reward is
in the doing. Whether gathering your brood
around the kitchen table for a joint project or
snatching a moment alone to create a surprise
for another member of your household, you'll
find the result is almost certain to be
appreciated. Gifts from the kitchen deserve
special consideration because for almost
everyone, food equals love, and that, of
course, is what Christmas is all about.

HANDMADE CARDS

Rubber stamps, either store-bought or custom-made, make decorating cards, gifts, and wraps so much easier. Use different-colored ink pads for the most effective results.

67 ⚜ News Update

Last year's Christmas card was likely the last time most of the people on your list heard from you. This year create a one-page newsletter or mini journal chronicling the activities and achievements of each member of the family. Add black-and-white photos if you wish. If your computer has graphics capability, use it to dress up the final product. Otherwise, make use of rubber stamps, decals, or artwork by the kids. Take the original to a copy shop for copying.

68 ⚜ Four for a Dollar

Those appalling four-for-a-dollar photos from a self-service photo booth can be turned into a memorable Christmas greeting. Pile the family, including the family dog, into the booth and take your best shots. Photocopy the pictures (do not cut apart) onto card stock, then let your imagination be your guide. Using colored felt-tip pens, draw silly expressions, mustaches, Groucho eyebrows, funny hats, and dangling earrings on everyone in the photo. Mail it just as a postcard, if you wish.

69 ⚜ Photo Montage

Make a montage of recent family photos taken on vacation or at special events and have it copied onto card stock. Write your message on the other side and put it into an envelope or use it as a postcard.

70 🎄 Ornamental Christmas Card

Create a Christmas card ornament using a piece of 8½- x 11-inch handmade paper in a soft color, four four-inch-long twigs, quarter-inch-wide ribbon, dried flowers or potpourri, and a glue gun. Fold the piece of paper in four, carefully lining up the sides and bottom before creasing, then glue the halves together to make a "card." Write your greeting on the inside. Use the glue gun to connect the twigs in a frame; allow to dry. Wrap the ribbon around the twigs, securing the corners of the frame by winding the ribbon around and around in a zigzag motion. Attach to the front of the card with glue. In the center of the frame, draw a wreath with white glue and sprinkle it with dried flowers or potpourri; when it dries, attach a tiny bow or silk rosette at the lower right-hand corner of the wreath. Add a few dried flowers to the joints of the twig frame. Stick a ribbon loop onto the back of the card for hanging. If you mail this card, be sure to use a padded Jiffy bag; if you personally present it, slip it into a cellophane sleeve or closeable Baggie.

71 ❄ Family Post

A simple way to personalize your Christmas card is to have a photo of your family turned into a picture postcard. A photo shop will print your snapshot onto postcards; you just add your written message, address, and post. The stamp costs less than for a card in an envelope.

72 ❄ Cork Stamp Greetings

Make your own stamps with Christmas images and use them to turn out hand-decorated cards and invites. Draw a pattern on the wide end of a cork from a wine, champagne, or other bottle. Carefully cut away the cork from around the image, going down about a quarter of an inch into the cork. Stamp the cork onto a stamp pad (use an assortment of colors) and press down hard on drawing paper. Since the images are small, plan to make several different ones to make the cards more interesting.

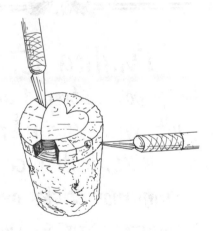

73 ❄ Sponge Stars

Cut kitchen sponges into star shapes, dip them into paint, and use them to decorate cards, wrapping paper, and invites.

74 ❧ Recipe Card: Mulled Cider

This Christmas greeting comes with a holiday recipe for mulled cider. You can use your own recipe and have a calligrapher create original artwork for you, or simply make a quality copy of our recipe below, and use it for your own card. Print on cream-toned textured stock, with your greeting and family name on the inside.

❧ Mulled Cider

In a large pot, steep 1 gallon of fresh apple cider with ¼ cup brown sugar, 12 whole cloves, 8 allspice berries, and 6 split cinnamon sticks over very low heat for 20 minutes. Stir in 1½ cups amber rum and ladle into mugs. Garnish each serving with a cinnamon stick. Makes 6 cups.

Mulled Cider

In a large pot, steep 1 gallon of fresh apple cider with ¼ cup brown sugar, 12 whole cloves, 8 allspice berries, and 6 split cinnamon sticks over very low heat for 20 minutes. Stir in 1½ cups amber rum and ladle into mugs. Garnish each serving with a cinnamon stick. Makes 6 cups

75 ✧ Glitter Greetings

Use pictures of trees, snow scenes, angels, doves, Santas, wreaths, stained glass windows, and stockings cut out of last year's Christmas cards, cherubs and hearts from Valentine's Day cards, and bits and pieces of old and broken jewelry as ingredients for homemade cards. Take a piece of 8½- X 11-inch handmade paper with rag edges, fold the sheet into four, and glue the image or images to the outside of your card. Take a few small pearls, beads, and colored rhinestones and glue them down for a glittering touch. In place of the stones you can outline all or part of the image (Santa's hat and buttons or the angel's wings, for example) with glue and pour on glitter.

HANDMADE PARTY INVITES

76 ✧ Perpetual Invite

If you host an annual holiday party or dinner, eliminate the bother of having to ponder new invites every year; after all, the dates don't change. Choose a timeless quote that you can use year after year, such as this one from the Bible:

> *Be not forgetful to entertain strangers;*
> *For thereby some have entertained angels unawares.*

> —New Testament, Hebrews 13:2

Vary the invitation from year to year by enclosing a different flat tree ornament. With the example above, an angel would be an appropriate choice.

77 ✧ Personal Stamp

Invest in a handcrafted rubber stamp to make the creation of an invitation a simple task.

78 🎋 A Message from the Art

Art postcards depicting seasonal themes, both secular and religious, make attractive invites. Museum gift shops have large stocks of these cards as do stores specializing in art books.

79 🎋 Inexpensive Dress Up

Use Christmas stickers to dress up plain notepaper for invites or thank-you cards.

80 🎋 Ring Out the Old

Distinguish your New Year's party invite from all the rest by including a handful of confetti.

81 🎋 Handmade Gifts

When you give someone a gift you've made yourself, you give of yourself. Big or small, a handmade gift is a personal expression of caring.

- Button Bracelet—Victorian young ladies used to make a "charm string." Not until she put the thousandth button on the string would the maiden marry. Vintage buttons make one-of-a-kind, easy-to-create pieces of jewelry. Thread a twelve-inch length of heavy elastic through the holes of assorted buttons. Measure the bracelet on your wrist, making sure it will fit over the hand, then finish off with a double knot; cut off the excess elastic. To make earrings to match, glue together two clusters of buttons and attach them to ear clips.
- Button Covers—Button covers for blouses and sweaters have become popular fashion accessories. Use vintage buttons in different styles and shapes but the same color to make a set of

six covers as a gift. Attach the buttons with a glue gun to closures from a crafts or notions store.

82 🐦 Button & Buckle Brooch

Vintage Bakelite buckles are often found at flea markets. They can be combined with old buttons in coordinated colors and shapes to make nostalgic-looking brooches to wear on a jacket lapel or at the collar of a high-necked blouse. You'll need two buttons per buckle, one big enough to cover the buckle's holes but smaller than the buckle itself. Glue that button on top of the buckle and glue a smaller button on top of that. The smaller button should have some sort of design carved into it—flowers, birds, or a cameo portrait. Allow the glue to dry, then attach a pin to the back of the brooch.

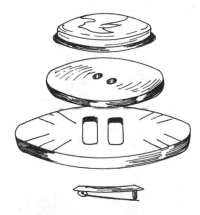

83 🐾 A Family Tree

This gift to a family member may well become a treasured heirloom. The number of branches depends on who the tree is for—parents or grandparents—and how many children and grandchildren they had. The one we do (for sixteen descendants) uses thirty-two pieces of eighteen-inch-long paper-covered wire.

About two inches from the bottom and going about six inches up, twist all of the pieces together. Fan the bottom pieces out to form the "roots" of the tree. At the top of the twist, begin to divide the "branches" into groups of four, fanning them out on both sides of the tree. Separate the strands of each group of four and fan them out as well. When you are done arranging the wire, take scissors and trim all around to form a tree

shape. Take color or black-and-white photos of each family member to be included and cut them into squares, ovals, or circles, about one and a half inches in size. Make a frame for each photo with potpourri or dried flowers. First, attach a loop of two-inch-long cord or ribbon to the top of the photo with a dollop of glue. Then draw a border of glue around the photo and sprinkle potpourri or dried rosebuds, delphiniums, and bits of heather onto the glue; allow to dry. Tie each photo to the tree in generational order. Take a six-inch square of one-and-a-half-inch-thick green Styrofoam and cover it with sheet moss. Stick the "roots" of the tree into the Styrofoam. Place a larger photo of the people you are honoring with this gift, also framed with dried flowers, at the base of the tree. For an evergreen effect, glue boxwood leaves to the branches and decorate the base with the remaining dried flowers. Use snow confetti for a more wintery look.

84 ⚡ Gilded Fruit Basket

This fruit basket makes a lovely hostess gift.

Figs, kiwis, and lady apples
Egg whites
3 sheets 18-karat gold leaf
  (available at craft stores)
Q-tips
Small woven wicker basket

Brown paper bags, shredded
Walnuts and pistachios in the
  shell
Cellophane wrap
3-inch-wide gold or white ribbon

   1. Using a pastry brush, paint the fruit with the egg white. Delicately pick up a bit of the gold leaf with a Q-tip. Dab the fruit with the gold leaf (which will break into an attractive random pattern).

   2. Fill the basket with shredded brown paper. Place the fruit in the basket and garnish with walnuts and pistachios.

   3. Finish with cellophane wrap gathered at the top with a large bow.

85 ❦ Fragrant Firestarters

Anyone who has a fireplace will be delighted to receive several of these fragrant firestarters. It's a much prettier way to start a fire than crumpled newspaper. Gather together six- to eight-inch-long pieces of pine and balsa branches, some dried heather and lavender, as well as small bunches of rosemary and thyme. Add three long cinnamon sticks and tie it all together with raffia, finishing in a bow. For a seasonal touch, glue a cluster of several little pinecones to the bow.

86 ❦ Recyclable Hostess Basket

This dried flower and moss basket can be used again and again. Immerse sheet moss in water to make it pliable, apply it in sections to a basket using a glue gun. Allow each section to dry before adding another. Then glue dried roses and heather to the rim of the basket, adding a few small pinecones. Fill with a mélange of seasonal fruit and nuts.

87 ❦ A Meaningful Calendar

To make a calendar with special meaning for a family member, start with a wall calendar given to you by a bank, dry cleaner, or airline. Choose twelve family photos, preferably ones commemorating such special occasions as birthdays, a christening, or a wedding. Make a color photocopy of each photo, the same size as the illustrations on the calendar. Using rubber cement, paste the photo on the month in which the pictured occasion took place.

88 🎀 Ribbon Pillow

While you were making the rounds of flea markets during the summer, perhaps you found some antique ribbon. If not, buy a selection of beautiful ribbons that anyone would love to live with to make this pillow.

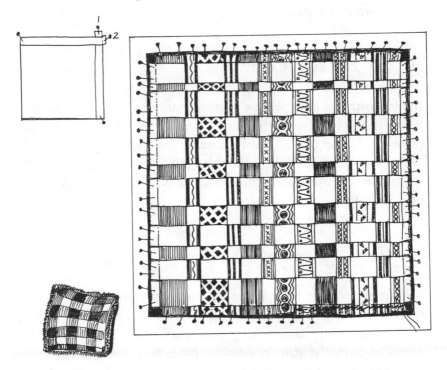

To make a twelve-inch pillow, work with ribbons thirteen inches long. Cut two thirteen-inch squares of solid color fabric. Attach the fabric with push pins to a board. At the upper left corner of the fabric, place one ribbon going horizontally and another vertically. Using a traditional basket weave, add ribbons along the top and side, weaving them in and out till you have completed the square. Pin the ribbons to the fabric, then lift off the board. Sew the ribbons down and attach the second piece of fabric as backing. Sew on color-coordinated cording all the way around, leaving an opening. Add a pillow and stitch the opening closed.

89 ⚑ Black & White Memories

Nothing is more evocative of times past than a black-and-white photograph. Everyone has a shoebox or drawer full of old photos. Choose one that has special meaning for the recipient. An inexpensive frame, preferably black or silver, turns even a fading photo into an heirloom.

90 ⚑ Button Frames

Individualize an inexpensive picture frame by using a glue gun to attach old buttons in different shapes and sizes on the corners of or all around the wooden frame. If the picture is black-and-white, you can use black and white buttons; if the picture is in color, color-coordinated ones. For baby pictures, use blue or pink buttons.

91 ⚑ A Puzzlement

Mount an enlarged photo of yourself or your family onto a piece of foam board. Cover the photo with a piece of tracing paper and lightly draw the jigsaw pattern, creating as many pieces of puzzle as you choose (the more pieces, the more difficult the puzzle). Using an X-ACTO knife, carefully cut through the photo and board along the pencil lines. Separate the pieces and place in a box.

92 ⚑ Found Objects

The ingredients of simple gifts often can be found around the house, especially when you want to find something to delight a little girl. Take a shoe box and glue flowered wrapping paper over it inside and out. Then look through your drawers and gather together all of the costume jewelry you have not worn for years. Fill the box and tie it up with a pretty hair ribbon.

93 🖉 Getting It Covered

Fabric-covered frames to hold a mirror or photo make great gifts and are simple to make. Take a wooden frame without grooves or carving on it and choose a piece of fabric at least one inch wider all around than the frame you are covering. Remove the backing and glass from your frame and lay it front side down on your piece of fabric (wrong side up). Work on top of a magazine or other layer of nonsmudge paper. Cut a small wedge out of the fabric at each corner so that each side of the fabric will fold over the frame separately. Spread white glue all around the outer rim of the back of the frame and wrap the material around the frame, making sure it is taut. Press with your fingers until dry. Then, using an X-ACTO blade, cut the fabric away from the inside of the frame, leaving a half-inch border all around. Spread the glue along the back of the frame and press until the fabric adheres. Cover the back of the frame with a matching or contrasting fabric, if you like.

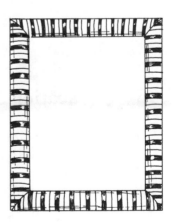

94 🖉 Travel Collage

A travel collage is a long-lasting visual reminder of a vacation well spent. Start with a piece of art paper the size of the collage you want to make and a frame the same size (an acrylic box frame works well here). Also buy some bold-colored mat paper; for a more fanciful creation you can also use small white or gold doilies. Gather all of the souvenir paper items you have from your vacation (for suggestions see page 13) as well as one or two of the best photos of you and your travel companion and spread them out. Arrange the items chronologically or on a map, cutting out arrows from the map to lead the eye from one vaca-

tion highlight to another. Or take a crazy quilt approach, placing the items in a haphazard but visually interesting way, using the mat paper or doilies as background. Paste down the items and the background pieces one by one on the art paper. Allow to dry and then frame.

95 🖈 Vacation Memory Box

Using the same type of materials as in the collage, take an old wooden or cardboard box with an attached lid (a cigar box is perfect) and create a three-dimensional record of your trip. As you lay out your collage, remember that the box is meant to stand open. Glue foreign money or stamps or seashells on the edges of the box and lid, hang a room key or souvenir key chain from the top, or trim the whole box with cutouts from road or street maps. The interior of the box should have at least one photo. If you have one with a view from your hotel window, use bits of lace to create "curtains" on either side of the picture. What you use and how you put it together is highly personal; that's why a memory box is such a special gift for a travel companion.

96   Decoupage Box

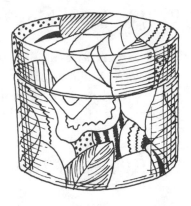

Decoupage is a good way to embellish a new box or recycle an old one. You can use the same technique to cover the top of a small table, a wooden or plastic tray, a plastic planter or vase, or any stone object. Start by assembling pictures cut out from old greeting cards, magazines, seed and flower catalogs, wallpaper, or wrapping paper. (If you use magazine or catalog pictures, spray them with fixative first to make them colorfast.)

Paper cutouts
2 paper cups
Elmer's glue
1 or 2 small brushes
Wooden or plastic box or other
   object

Small piece of clean kitchen
   sponge
Clear acrylic spray or varnish
   (Liquitex gloss polymer spray
   or liquid)

1. Gather the cutouts and lay them out on the table in the design you want to have on the finished product. Fill 1 cup with water and the other with a squirt of glue diluted with a few drops of water. (The glue should be thinned only enough to paint on. Test by painting a scrap of paper; if the glue beads it needs thickening.) Apply glue to the cutouts, one by one, and lay them down on the box, overlapping in an attractive design. (If the cutouts are not to overlap, apply the glue directly to the box.) Once the cutouts are in place, press down gently with your fingers. With a damp sponge, carefully wipe off the excess glue. Allow to dry overnight. Do not apply the finish until the glue is completely dry.

2. For the finish, use either clear acrylic spray or Liquitex gloss, which is painted on. For a wood box, apply 15 to 20 coats, letting each coat dry completely before applying the next. Apply 3 coats at most in 1 day. A plastic box requires only 3 to 5 coats to finish.

97 🖋 Something to Brag About

Grandparents love to brag about their grandchildren's accomplishments. Make a scrapbook especially for them that contains some school projects, honors, mementos, recent photos, and a personal note from the children.

98 🖋 Bistro Tray

Take a baking tray or cookie sheet and glue on canceled foreign stamps and domestic commemorative stamps. Add some wine labels and a few cigar bands, if you can find any. Cover the entire tray, then apply several coats of polyurethane varnish (see page 55).

99 🖋 Lacy Heart

This easy-to-make decorative gift makes use of a staple of Christmas, the candy cane. Buy a two-and-a-half-yard piece of four-inch-wide ruffled lace edging that has a casing on the back at least half an inch wide. If you want to use a piece of old lace, add a casing starting half an inch from the plain edge. Cut the piece of lace in half. Insert a long candy cane into each piece,

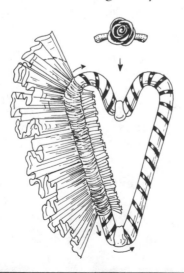

gathering the ruffle as you go. With a glue gun, attach the candy canes at the top and bottom to form a heart. When it dries, attach a tiny silk rose at the point where the candy cane heart dips and glue a ribbon loop at the back for hanging. You can also make a miniature version of this lacy heart, using tiny candy canes, to hang on a Victorian-style tree.

FOOD FOR THOUGHTFULNESS

Delight your friends and family with cakes, chutney, cream liqueurs, and homemade candy from your kitchen. Make the gift of food more special with inventive wrapping, see page 76 for suggestions.

100 ⁋ Cranberry Apple Chutney

PREP: 5 minutes   COOK: 20 to 25 minutes
MAKES: about 4 cups

The busy cook will be grateful to have your chutney on hand to serve with a traditional turkey dinner.

1 (12-ounce) bag cranberries
1 cup sugar
1 cup orange juice
1 apple, peeled and sliced
½ cup currants or raisins
1 cinnamon stick

1. Place all ingredients in a large nonreactive saucepan. Bring to a boil, stirring to dissolve sugar. Reduce heat to medium and simmer 20 minutes, or until cranberries have burst.
2. Remove cinnamon stick and spoon into 4 sterilized half-pint or 2 pint jars. Cover and refrigerate for up to 3 weeks.

101   Pumpkin Spice Jar Cakes

PREP: 20 minutes   BAKE: 40 minutes   MAKES: 8 cakes

1 stick (4 ounces) plus 3 tablespoons unsalted butter, softened
3½ cups light brown sugar
4 eggs
2 cups pureed cooked or canned
  pumpkin
3⅓ cups flour

1½ teaspoons baking powder
1 teaspoon baking soda
1 teaspoon cinnamon
½ teaspoon ground ginger
¼ teaspoon ground mace
1 cup chopped walnuts (about
  4 ounces)

1. Preheat oven to 325°F. Before starting batter, wash 8 (1-pint) wide-mouth canning jars with lids in hot, soapy water and let them drain, dry, and cool to room temperature. Generously grease insides of jars.

2. With an electric mixer, beat together butter and about half of brown sugar until light and fluffy. Beat in eggs, then remaining sugar. Beat in pumpkin. Set aside.

3. Sift together flour, baking powder, baking soda, cinnamon, ginger, and mace. Gradually add to pumpkin mixture in thirds, beating well after each addition to make a thick batter. Stir in walnuts.

4. Spoon 1 level cupful of batter into each jar. Carefully wipe rims clean, then place jars in the center of preheated oven. Bake 40 minutes.

5. About 10 minutes before cakes are done, bring a medium saucepan of water to a boil. Put in jar lids, cover, and remove from heat. Keep lids in hot water until they're used.

6. When cakes are done, remove jars from oven one at a time. If jar rims need cleaning, use a moistened paper towel. Carefully put lids and rings in place, then screw tops tightly shut. Place jars on a wire rack; they will seal as they cool.

102 ✦ Piña Colada Jar Cakes

PREP: 20 minutes BAKE: 40 minutes MAKES: 8 cakes

1 (20-ounce) can unsweetened crushed pineapple
1 stick (4 ounces) plus 3 tablespoons unsalted butter, softened
3½ cups packed light brown sugar
4 eggs
½ cup dark rum
3⅓ cups flour
1½ teaspoons baking powder
1 teaspoon baking soda
1 cup sweetened flaked coconut

1. Preheat oven to 325°F. Before starting batter, wash 8 (1-pint) wide-mouth canning jars with lids in hot, soapy water and let them drain, dry, and cool to room temperature. Generously grease insides of jars.

2. Drain crushed pineapple for about 10 minutes in a colander, reserving juice. Puree drained pineapple in a food processor. Measure out 1½ cups puree, adding a little juice if necessary to make 1½ cups. Set puree aside. Discard remaining juice or reserve for another use.

3. With an electric mixer, beat together butter and half of brown sugar until light and fluffy. Beat in eggs, then remaining sugar. Beat in pineapple puree and rum and set aside.

4. Sift together flour, baking powder, and baking soda. Gradually add to pineapple mixture in thirds, beating well after each addition to make a thick batter. Stir in coconut.

5. Spoon 1 level cupful of batter into each jar. Carefully wipe

(continued on next page)

rims clean, then place jars in center of preheated oven. Bake 40 minutes.

6. About 10 minutes before cakes are done, bring a medium saucepan of water to a boil. Put in jar lids, cover, and remove from heat. Keep lids in hot water until they're used.

7. When cakes are done, remove jars from oven. If jar rims need cleaning, use a moistened paper towel. Carefully put lids and rings in place, then screw tops tightly shut. Place jars on a wire rack; they will seal as they cool.

103 ⁂ Chocolate Applesauce Jar Cakes

PREP: 20 minutes   BAKE: 40 minutes   MAKES: 8 cakes

1 stick (4 ounces) plus 3 tablespoons unsalted butter, softened
3 cups sugar
4 eggs
1 tablespoon vanilla extract
1 teaspoon almond extract
2 cups unsweetened applesauce

3 cups flour
¾ cup unsweetened cocoa powder
1 teaspoon baking soda
½ teaspoon baking powder
⅛ teaspoon salt
½ cup finely chopped pecans

1. Preheat oven to 325°F. Before starting batter, wash 8 (1-pint) wide-mouth canning jars with lids in hot, soapy water and let them drain, dry, and cool to room temperature. Generously grease insides of jars.

2. With an electric mixer, beat together butter and half of sugar until light and fluffy. Beat in eggs, then remaining sugar, vanilla, and almond extract. Beat in applesauce.

3. Sift together flour, cocoa powder, baking soda, baking powder, and salt. Add to applesauce mixture in thirds, beating well after each addition to make a thick batter. Stir in chopped pecans.

4. Spoon 1 level cupful of batter into each jar. Carefully wipe rims clean, then place jars in center of preheated oven. Bake 40 minutes.

5. About 10 minutes before cakes are done, bring a medium saucepan of water to a boil. Put in jar lids, cover, and remove from heat. Keep lids in hot water until they're used.

6. When cakes are done, remove jars from oven. If jar rims need cleaning, use a moistened paper towel. Carefully put lids and rings in place, then screw tops tightly shut. Place jars on a wire rack; they will seal as they cool.

104 ⚞ Dark Fruitcake

PREP: 30 minutes   BAKE: 1¾ to 2¼ hours
MAKES: 7 small or 3 regular loaves

Here's a fruitcake for those who want a bit more cake with their fruit. Honey, molasses, and chopped dates give this rich, dark cake unusual smoothness and moisture.

1 pound mixed diced candied fruit
    (fruitcake mix)
1 (15-ounce) box raisins
½ pound chopped pitted dates
1 cup slivered almonds (4 ounces)
1¾ to 2 cups brandy
2 cups sifted flour
½ teaspoon baking soda
¼ teaspoon cinnamon

¼ teaspoon ground cloves
¼ teaspoon ground mace
2 sticks (8 ounces) unsalted but-
    ter, softened
1 cup packed dark brown sugar
5 eggs
½ cup honey
½ cup molasses

1. Preheat oven to 275°F. Generously butter 7 small foil loaf pans (5¾ X 3¼ X 2 inches) or 3 regular-size foil loaf pans (8 X 3¾ X 2½ inches). Line bottom of each pan with wax paper.

2. In a very large bowl, combine candied fruit, raisins, dates, almonds, and ¼ cup brandy. Set aside. Sift together flour, baking soda, cinnamon, cloves, and mace. Set aside.

3. In a medium bowl, beat butter and brown sugar until light and fluffy. Beat in eggs one at a time. Beat in honey and molasses. Pour over fruits and almonds and mix well. Add flour mixture to fruit in thirds, mixing well after each addition.

4. Spoon batter into prepared pans so each is about two-thirds full. Place in upper third of preheated oven. Put a shallow pan

(continued on next page)

filled with water on bottom shelf. Bake cakes 1 hour; remove pan of water. Continue to bake cakes 45 to 60 minutes longer for small, 1 to 1¼ hours for regular, until a toothpick stuck into center of a cake comes out clean and edges begin to pull away from sides of pan.

6. When cakes are done, let them cool in their pans on a wire rack. Sprinkle tops of cakes with brandy—about 2 tablespoons each for small cakes, ¼ cup for regular. Wrap tightly in foil or plastic wrap and place in tins or containers with tight-fitting lids. If possible, age cakes 3 to 4 weeks; moisten each with 1 to 2 tablespoons brandy at least twice more before serving.

105 🥃 Athol Brose

PREP: 5 minutes   COOK: 5 to 7 minutes   MAKES: about 3 pints

Athol, where this brew originated, is a district in central Scotland once famous for its deer hunting; "brose" is a Scottish word for "broth." Early versions of this old favorite included water in which oatmeal had been soaked overnight. Here gelatin provides the thickening.

1½ teaspoons unflavored gelatin   *3 cups heavy cream*
⅓ cup cold water   *3 cups Scotch whisky*
1 cup honey

1. In a small saucepan, sprinkle the gelatin over water and let soften for several minutes. Place over low heat and cook, stirring occasionally, until gelatin dissolves, 1 to 2 minutes. Remove from heat and set aside.

2. In a large saucepan, heat honey over medium-low heat until thin, about 2 minutes. Stir in cream and heat until mixture is quite warm (about 110°F), 2 to 3 minutes. Stir in gelatin mixture. Remove from heat and stir in whisky.

3. Serve warm or chilled. Store brose in a sterilized bottle in refrigerator, where it will keep for a month or more. If giving as a gift, put in an old-fashioned bottle, wrapped in fabric (see page 74).

106 ⚞ Creamsicle Liqueur

PREP: 5 minutes   COOK: 5 minutes   MAKES: about 3½ cups

The orange and vanilla flavors of the old-time Creamsicle show up here in a more sophisticated guise. Like the other cream liqueurs, this is a rich, heady brew that goes a long way.

1 teaspoon unflavored gelatin
¼ cup cold water
1 (14-ounce) can sweetened con-
    densed milk

1 cup heavy cream
1¼ cups 80-proof vodka
1 tablespoon vanilla extract
2 teaspoons orange extract

1. In a small saucepan, sprinkle gelatin over water and let soften for several minutes. Place over low heat and cook, stirring occasionally, until gelatin dissolves, 1 to 2 minutes. Remove from heat and set aside.

2. In a medium saucepan, combine condensed milk and cream. Heat until quite warm (about 110°F), 2 to 3 minutes. Stir in the gelatin mixture. Remove from heat and stir in vodka, vanilla, and orange extract.

3. Pour into a sterilized bottle and refrigerate for 1 to 2 days before using. Shake well before serving in liqueur or cordial glasses. This mixture will keep in refrigerator for a month or longer. For gift-giving, wrap the bottle in fabric (see page 74).

107 ⚞ Rum and Maple Cream Liqueur

PREP: 5 minutes   COOK: 5 minutes   MAKES: about 4 cups

1 teaspoon unflavored gelatin
2 tablespoons cold water
1 cup maple syrup
1 cup heavy cream

1 (5-ounce) can evaporated milk
1 cup 80-proof dark rum
1 teaspoon vanilla extract

(continued on next page)

1. In a small saucepan, sprinkle gelatin over water and let soften several minutes. Place over low heat and cook, stirring occasionally, until gelatin dissolves. Remove from heat and set aside.

2. In a heavy medium saucepan, combine maple syrup, cream, and evaporated milk. Place over medium-low heat and cook until mixture is quite warm (about 110°F), 2 or 3 minutes. Stir in gelatin mixture. Remove from heat and stir in rum and vanilla.

3. Pour into a sterilized bottle and refrigerate for 1 to 2 days before using. Shake well before serving in liqueur or cordial glasses. This mixture will keep in refrigerator a month or longer. Wrap the bottle in fabric (see page 74).

108 🦌 Christmas Toffee

PREP: 15 minutes   COOK: 10 to 12 minutes   CHILL: 1½ hours
MAKES: 20 (1–inch) squares

A gift of homemade candy is truly a gift from the heart, and no one needs to know how easily this one was made. Wrap Christmas toffee in clear cellophane tied with a crisp tartan plaid bow.

2 cups sliced almonds (about 8 ounces)
12 ounces milk chocolate or semi-sweet chocolate chips (2 cups)
2 sticks (8 ounces) butter, cut into bits
1½ cups packed light brown sugar

1. Preheat oven to 325°F. Spread out almonds on a baking sheet and bake, stirring occasionally, until lightly browned, 5 to 7 minutes. Let cool.

2. Coarsely chop chocolate chips in a food processor, pulsing on and off. Transfer to a medium bowl. In same processor bowl, coarsely chop almonds, pulsing on and off. Add to chocolate chips, tossing to combine. Spread half of mixture evenly over bottom of a well-greased 13- x 9-inch baking pan.

3. In a heavy medium saucepan, bring butter and brown sugar

to a boil, stirring constantly, over medium heat. Cook 5 to 7 minutes, or until syrup is light golden-brown and just reaches the hard crack stage (300°F on a candy thermometer). At that point, a bit of syrup, when dropped into a bowl of ice water, should separate into threads that are hard and brittle.

4. Pour hot syrup evenly over nut mixture. Top with remaining nut mixture, smoothing and pressing down gently with a spatula. Refrigerate until toffee is set and chocolate is firm, about 1½ hours. Cut into squares or irregular pieces. Store in a tightly covered container in refrigerator up to 2 weeks.

109 🐿 Bourbon Balls

PREP: 15 minutes   COOK: none   MAKES: about 5 dozen

This recipe is a traditional Christmas standby, but it is new to every generation. Bourbon balls improve if they are allowed to mellow for at least a week, and they can be made up to one month in advance. Attractively packaged in a tin or other airtight container, they make a great edible gift.

1 (9-ounce) box vanilla wafer cookies
3 cups powdered sugar
⅔ cup bourbon
⅓ cup corn syrup
⅓ cup unsweetened cocoa powder
½ pound shelled pecans (about 2 cups)

1. In a food processor, combine vanilla wafers, 2 cups powdered sugar, bourbon, corn syrup, and cocoa powder. Process until cookies are ground to crumbs and mixture is evenly blended.

2. Add pecans and process, pulsing, until nuts are finely chopped. Turn out into a bowl.

3. Form mixture into 1-inch balls, rolling them between your palms until smooth. Dredge in remaining powdered sugar to coat. Store in an airtight container.

110 🖋 Chocolate Walnut Biscotti

PREP: 15 minutes   COOK: 1½ hours   MAKES: 4 dozen

These dry and very chocolatey cookies make excellent holiday gifts, as they keep well for weeks. Not-too-sweet biscotti are best dunked in a steaming cup of coffee or tea. Pack in an antique or reproduction tin, the perfect reusable gift wrap.

2 cups coarsely chopped walnuts
   (about 8 ounces)
2 cups flour
2 cups unsweetened cocoa powder
2 cups sugar
1 teaspoon baking powder
1 teaspoon baking soda
6 eggs
⅛ teaspoon salt
¼ cup brandy or coffee
2 teaspoons vanilla extract

1. Preheat oven to 325°F. Spread walnuts on a cookie sheet and toast in oven 5 to 8 minutes, shaking pan several times, until walnuts are light brown. Let cool. Lower oven temperature to 300°.

2. In a large bowl, combine flour, cocoa powder, sugar, baking powder, and baking soda. Stir or whisk gently until well mixed. Make a well in center.

3. In a medium bowl, beat eggs with salt until well blended. Mix in brandy and vanilla. Pour egg mixture into well in center of flour mixture. Beat together until a soft dough forms. Stir in toasted walnuts.

4. With lightly moistened hands, divide dough in half. On a parchment-lined baking sheet, shape dough into 2 loaves about 12 x 3½ x ½ inch. Bake 50 minutes, or until dough appears dry. Remove from oven and cut loaves into ½-inch-thick slices.

5. Arrange slices on baking sheet and bake 20 minutes. Turn over and bake 20 minutes longer, until firm and dry. Let cool. Store in an airtight container for up to several weeks.

CHAPTER 5

It's a Wrap!

Wrapping styles vary from bare minimum to extravaganza. There is nothing wrong with fancy wrap and ribbon—providing you buy it after the holidays the previous year at a deep discount, and that you find ways to recycle it. Consider also using wraps made from recyclables and those that will be recycled because they are part of the gift. The whole family can share in gift wrapping. It is a creative and imaginative way to experience the warmth and togetherness of the holidays.

MAKING YOUR OWN WRAPPINGS

Involve the kids in the holiday preparations by helping them make the wrapping paper for their gifts to grandma, a teacher, or their friends.

111 🐿 Rainbow Wrap

Use a lightweight wrapping paper, such as tableau paper, which you can buy in an art-supply store, or tissue paper. It will look as if it's been tie-dyed.

Water
Red, green, blue, and yellow food coloring

Muffin tin
Tableau paper or tissue paper, up to 24 inches square

1. Mix water and food coloring in the cups of a muffin tin, using less water for deeper hues, more for subtle shadings. Fill 1 cup with water only. Fold the paper into 2-inch-wide accordion folds one way, creasing the edges firmly. Then accordion fold it into squares or triangles.

2. Dip the corners of the folded paper into the coloring. You can do this two ways. Dip the corners into one or more different dye colors, dipping into water first, then into the dye for a more feathery look. Or alternate the techniques to get an even more interesting effect.

3. When finished dipping, blot the folded paper between several sheets of newspaper, pressing down hard. Remove the paper and carefully open. Let the paper dry on top of newspaper.

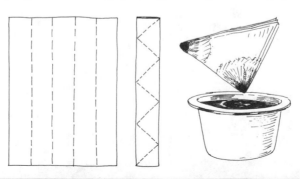

112 🖋 Leaf Wrap

Do this in late summer or fall with an assortment of fresh leaves. Place a leaf on a stamp pad and cover it with a piece of plastic wrap. Using your finger, gently rub over the plastic wrap to ink the leaf. Lift the plastic and remove the leaf, using tweezers if necessary. Place the leaf, ink side down, onto the wrapping paper and cover with a small piece of scrap paper. Gently rub to print the leaf. Use 1 large leaf or a variety of smaller leaves and create a design.

113 🖋 The Perfect Bow

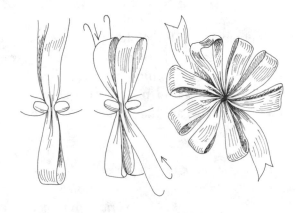

Make a loop with one end of a two-yard-long piece of ribbon, holding it in place with your fingers. Form another loop by bringing the remaining ribbon up and over where you are holding the ribbon in place. Make a third and fourth in the same manner. Pinch the center of the bow with your fingers and secure with wire or a narrow piece of matching ribbon. Spread the loops open into a bow. For a rosette bow resembling a flower, continue with the same method, forming several more loops.

114 🖋 Kid Wrapped

Ask your kids to choose what they would like to have on their very own wrapping paper. Perhaps a favorite drawing made during the school year (make sure it's signed), or a composition that earned an A. Have them paste whatever it is on plain legal-size paper. Make a copy, or if the package is big, several copies. Having the kids help with the copying is part of the fun.

115  Vegetable Prints

Here's an acceptable way for children to play with their food. Using fruits and vegetables to print on paper creates unique wraps and cards that kids enjoy making. Instead of tempera paints, they could use stamp pads with different-colored inks, but remember ink stains are harder to get out than water-based paints.

Butcher's paper, tissue paper, or shelf paper, 9 X 12 inches or larger
Newspapers
Jar of water
Paintbrushes
Various fruits and vegetables
Tempera paints

1. Arrange a work area with the paper spread on top of newspapers and a jar filled with water to hold your brushes. Take a mushroom, a cauliflower floret, a carrot, and an apple and cut them in half. Cut the mushroom and cauliflower from top to bottom; cut the apple crosswise and remove the seeds. Allow the halves to dry on a paper towel for at least an hour. You may also use orange and lemon halves, but they take at least 2 days to dry.

2. Brush the cut surface of the vegetable with tempera paint and print by pressing the vegetable firmly on the paper. You will be able to make 3 impressions before you need to repaint. Make a random pattern using several vegetables or make rows of the same vegetable in different colors. When the paint is dry, the paper is ready to use.

116 🖋 It's in the Bag

You could also metallize the bag with oil-based gold paint and splatter it à la Jackson Pollock.

Gold spray paint
Brown paper lunch or grocery bag
Gold tissue paper
Gold silk wire ribbon, 3 inches
  wide

3 long cinnamon sticks
Silk roses (optional)
Plastic flowers, sprayed gold
  (optional)
Glue gun (optional)

    1. Spray the paint on the bag in a hit-or-miss fashion. Wrap the gift in the tissue paper and place it in the bag, allowing the tissue to stick out the top of the bag.

    2. Tie the ribbon into a knot around the top of the bag. Place the cinnamon sticks on the knot, then tie the ribbon into a bow. For a fancier effect, instead of the cinnamon sticks attach a silk flower or 3 or 4 plastic ones to the bow using a glue gun.

117 ◈ Other Ways to Brown Bag It

- Use rubber stamps in Christmas motifs with red and green ink pads to decorate the bags.
- Use stencils of leaves and ivy. Fold over the top of the bag and start stenciling here so the leaves appear to be coming from inside the bag. Tie with raffia, adding a sprig of live pine or holly.
- Cut a sponge into small round pieces and using water and food coloring as in Rainbow Wrap (see page 68), dip the sponge into the colors and sponge-paint color onto the bags. Allow them to dry and fill with matching tissue paper.
- Cut a sponge into shapes such as trees, stars, or bells. Using water and food coloring as in Rainbow Wrap, sponge-paint the designs onto the paper bags.
- Punch holes in the top of a paper bag and thread raffia through them, finishing in a bow.

118 ◈ Kraft Paper

If your presents are boxed, buy a roll of brown kraft paper, the kind most commonly used for wrapping packages to mail. See above and pages 68–71 for ways to decorate the paper.

- Dress up a brown-paper-wrapped package by using a glue gun to attach dried hydrangeas, sprigs of bittersweet, and gold-sprayed pinecones.
- Draw pictures on your packages with white glue, then sprinkle fine glitter, multicolored foil confetti, sequins, or tiny stars on the design; allow all a few minutes to dry. For example, draw a tree with alternating rows of glitter and rows of red sequins.
- Let the little ones finger paint onto brown paper or plain white butcher paper and use that as wrapping paper for gifts.
- Draw a design with glue and attach green or red pasta shells, corkscrews, and tubes.
- Glue on real seashells collected last summer. Add raffia ties.

- Glue on pieces of colored felt in the shape of hearts, stars, and bells.
- Use pictures cut out from last year's Christmas cards to glue onto your package; cherubs, angels, trees, religious motifs, snow scenes, and stockings hung by the chimney are all colorful adornments.
- Buy sheets of pressure-sensitive type in a stationery or art store in several different styles—script, sans serif, bold, Gothic—and sizes to inscribe season's greetings on your package.
- Decorate plain paper packages with foil stars in many colors, gold notary seals, and bright color-coding label dots and strips, all from the stationery store.

119   Tissue Paper Flowers

To make tissue paper flowers for your packages, take several sheets of tissue and accordion fold them together lengthwise, making 2-inch-wide folds. Cut into a point at each end, then fold in the middle. Scrunch the paper together at the middle and wrap with a piece of tape. If you want to add a stem, insert a pipe cleaner before taping. Gently pull apart the "petals" of the flower. You may want to wrap with another bit of tape at this point to secure the flower's shape. Use white glue to attach the flowers to packages.

120   Nontraditional Wraps

- Wrap a silk scarf or handkerchiefs or a hard-to-pack small gift in parchment paper bought at an art-supply store. Roll the present in the parchment and tie it around the middle with a thin red or gold cord. Use sealing wax to seal the package.
- Stores that sell wallpaper usually have remnants or old sample books that you can buy. Wallpaper patterns can be beautiful and unusual, often with embossed or flocked designs.
- Instead of spending money for a box that will only be discarded, buy a flowered underbed storage box. Storage boxes

are inexpensive and easy to assemble; they will definitely be used long after Christmas is over. You can do the same with a hatbox.

• Use the empty cardboard rolls from toilet tissue or paper towels to wrap small stocking-stuffer gifts for a child. Cover the cardboard with foil paper, then wrap another piece of foil around it. Pinch the ends and tie at each end.

• Furoshiki, a centuries-old Japanese tradition, uses pieces of cloth to wrap gifts. Unlike wrapping paper, the furoshiki can be used over again. Use lightweight cloth to wrap a box or a bottle as shown in the illustrations below.

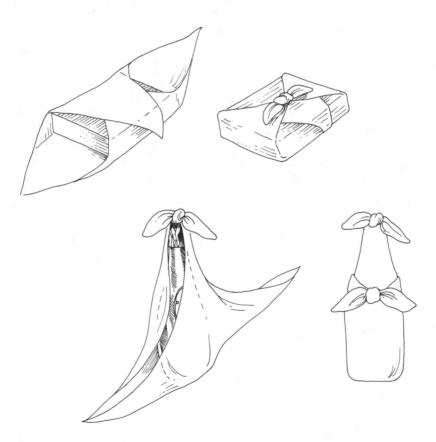

121 ⚞ More Fabric Wraps

• Tie a handkerchief-wrapped package with a piece of antique lace and tuck a new or old fabric flower into the knot.

- Tie a silk scarf wrap with a matching color wire-edged silk ribbon, then add some sprigs of lavender and a few cinnamon sticks for a fragrant finish.
- For a bandanna-wrapped present, use something rustic to finish the package off, raffia or a piece of rough packing cord tied into a bow.

122 🖋 A Gift with Strings Attached

Make a six-inch-tall fabric drawstring bag that can be recycled for use as a jewelry bag or makeup kit. Use silk or silky polyester or an interesting old piece of fabric.

1 piece fabric, 34 X 4 inches
1 piece fabric in another pattern,
   34 X 8 inches
1 circular piece, either fabric,
   5 inches in diameter
1 piece ribbon or cord, 36 inches
   long

1. Take the 4-inch-wide piece of fabric, fold the ends under ½ inch and stitch ¼ inch from the edge to finish.

2. To create the casing for drawstring, fold the long top edge of the same piece ¼ inch to wrong side and iron. Fold over again ¾ inch and stitch hem ¼ inch from folded edge.

3. Now with right sides facing center, pin together both pieces of the fabric with bottom edges even. To join the pieces sew a ½-inch seam; then open and iron flat. With right sides facing, join the short edges of the material and sew a ¾-inch seam starting at the raw edge and finishing 1½ inches from the casing. With right sides still facing, pin the remaining raw edge to the circle of fabric and stitch a ½-inch seam. Turn the bag right side out. Feed the trim or ribbon through the casing at the top and pull to close.

MORE RECYCLED WRAPS

123 ✒ All the Print That's Fit to Use

Instead of putting all of your newspapers out for recycling use newsprint as wrapping paper. Wrap housewares gifts in the classified section of the Sunday newspaper; use the stock-market pages to wrap gifts for executives on your list; and for children's presents, the Sunday comics. Buy Chinese, Russian, or Greek newspapers for added visual interest.

124 ✒ Map Wrap

Use a road or street map to wrap presents for the travelers on your gift list. You need only look in the glove compartment of your car or to the memorabilia collected on last year's vacation.

125 ✒ Sock It to 'Em

Buy a pair of whimsical socks to use as wrapping for a series of small presents. Tie the socks together with a big wire-edged bow.

126 ✒ Wraps for Food Gifts

- Wrap homebaked gifts in cellophane or tissue paper and place in terra-cotta pots, baskets, or Shaker boxes, which can be reused.
- For homemade food gifts in jars and bottles, tie one or two checked cloth napkins around the top of the jar with ribbon or raffia. Tuck a small utensil like measuring spoons or a tiny wooden scoop in the bow.
- Use cotton dishtowels or cloth napkins to wrap presents of homebaked breads and cakes. If you're giving several breads and cakes, tie them all together in a small checked tablecloth.

- Fill a metal, plastic, or wicker lunch box with homebaked cookies.
- Fill a string bag with small presents or present it as the gift of a picnic by filling with a wedge of cheese, an apple, and a bottle of wine. A string bag is a useful and ecologically sound gift that keeps on giving.

127 🌱 Decorative Flower Basket

Put fragrant soaps in an oval grass basket and glue or staple on a bunch of old or new fabric flowers to the lid. The basket makes a decorative addition to any bathroom.

For a seasonal variation on this basket loop a piece of red and green plaid ribbon around a few cinnamon sticks and glue the ribbon in a diagonal to the lid of the basket. Glue several miniature pinecones around the cinnamon sticks.

GIFT TIES

Whatever is used to tie a gift should be saved and reused. Wherever possible, ribbon, cords, tags, or cards should not be discarded.

128 🌱 Glittering Prize

For a positively glowing presentation, tie a string of battery-powered white lights around the package instead of a ribbon.

129 🌱 Fit to Be Trimmed

Seek out a decorator fabric shop, retail trimming store, or sewing supplies store and look for braids, cordings, tiebacks, fringes, and tassels to use instead of ribbon. Almost all can be used later on for curtains, for keys, or as belts.

130 ⚜ Ribbon Redux

If you must buy ribbon, choose French, handembroidered, or handwoven ribbon beautiful enough to be recycled as hair ribbons by the ladies of the house. Also look for antique ribbon at flea markets and antique shops.

131 ⚜ All Tied Up

Use one or two pairs of colored or patterned shoelaces with jingle bells attached to tie up small packages.

132 ⚜ Buttoned Bows

Thread an unusual vintage or new button onto wire and attach it to the center of the bow on a package.

TAGS

Use your imagination and you will never spend money for a gift tag again.

133 ⚜ Double Duty Cards

Use the front part of last year's Christmas cards as this year's gift tags. Just check that there is no writing on the other side.

134 ⚜ Nostalgic Bits & Pieces

Combine old-fashioned nostalgic images cut from old cards and glue them to small round, heart-shape, square, or rectangular white or gold doilies and glue them to the package as tags.

135 🖋 Photo ID

Instead of writing the name of the recipient on the present, use a very old photo of that person as the gift tag. Mount it onto a piece of card stock or lightweight cardboard, then punch a hole in it and use ribbon or raffia to attach. Kids just love to distribute the gifts, trying to match the childhood photo to an older family member.

136 🖋 Econo Tags

This is a truly economical bit of recycling. Cut tags out of a manila file folder (see pages 261 and 262 for patterns) and add gold stars or glitter.

137 🖋 Yummy Tags

Make edible cookie tags to put on gift packages from your children or for other children. Use animal or Christmas motif cutters or use the patterns on pages 261 and 262 to cut out cookies in the form of tags. Use icing to write the name of the recipient (see page 189 for recipe).

138 🖋 From the Kitchen of . . .

Invest in a rubber stamp that personalizes homebaked or handmade presents by indicating they come from your kitchen or were created by you. If you make a lot of gifts, this is something nice to give yourself.

139 🖋 Elegant Fabric Boxes

Collect an assortment of boxes large and small and use glue to cover them with rich paisley and plaid fabrics. Add velvet ties and braided trims.

140   Berry Boxed

Save the boxes that strawberries come in and use them as gift boxes for homemade cookies. Weave gingham or plaid ribbon through the slats, put in some colored tissue paper, and wrap it all up in clear cellophane.

141   Cheese Boxed

Design your own decorative box to hold a gift of jewelry by gluing loose pearls and beads to cover the lid of a cheese box (from the dairy section of the supermarket). You can also make designs using gumdrops, Life Savers, and red-hots.

142   Canned Cans

Soup cans can be used to wrap loose holiday candies or to hold a gift of Christmas flowers. Wash the can and peel off the label. Using a glue gun, attach cinnamon sticks or candy canes to cover the can completely. Tie a festive bow around the middle.

143 🖋 The Incredible Edible Box

The ultimate recyclable box for a small lightweight present is made of graham crackers or Social Tea biscuits held together with icing and decorated with icing, colored sprinkles, and dragées.

SECOND GIFT WRAP

Skip the traditional paper and ribbons and make the container a part of the gift.

144 🖋 Baskets

Baskets come in all sizes and shapes, with or without handles and lids, and they make attractive containers for gifts. Packing your gifts in baskets doubles the pleasure as most will see reuse as picnic hampers; holders for bread, potpourri, guest towels, or bills; or simply as decorative accessories in a country kitchen. Wrap your goodies-filled baskets with cellophane and tie with wire-edged ribbon.

145   Tins

Antique and reproduction tins make useful and decorative additions to any kitchen. They are ideal for packing such food gifts as gourmet coffees and teas, spices, candy, cookies, and cakes, and they will most likely continue to be used. Next year you can give the person refills for last year's tin.

146   Jars

A mason jar is the perfect container for homemade condiments, preserves, or store-bought candies, or even biscuits for the dog of the house (see page 39). Tie a red-and-white cloth napkin around the top and secure with a plaid or gingham taffeta bow.

147   The Art of Wrap

You don't have to be rich to have a Van Gogh or a Matisse under your tree. Place presents in reproduction shopping bags stuffed with copious amounts of tissue paper peeking out the top. The bags, available at museum shops and large gift and novelty shops, are an attractive alternative to wrapping paper, and they are sturdy enough to reuse as totes.

148   Don't Scrap It!

Take scraps of fancy wrapping paper too small to use on their own, overlap the pieces into an attractive square or rectangular shaped collage, and glue them together. Use this to wrap your packages.

PART THREE

Decorating the Home & Garden

CHAPTER 6

Wreaths, Garlands, Swags . . . & a Glimpse of Stockings

The eye becomes magically selective during the Christmas season. Worn carpets recede, and all that is festive and bright comes to the fore. Homes are transformed. Whether you like your holidays plain or fancy, there are easy ways to achieve a holiday look. How you do that tells as much about you as your signature. It's what you, your family, and your guests will remember long after the holidays have passed.

149 ❧ Look First

First decide which are the main areas to decorate for the season's events. If you have a big country-style eat-in kitchen, decorations there are a must. In a city apartment, the living room and dining room are the likely choices. In a brownstone or town house, in addition to the dining room, there are the parlor and the library too. And don't forget the doors of the upstairs bedrooms if that's where guests will be putting their coats or using the bathroom. If the guest room has a four-poster, for example tie generous satin ribbons around each post; set a bowl of fragrant potpourri and a candle next to the bed; and always place a fragrant candle or a small floral arrangement in each of the bathrooms.

NATURE GUIDE

Wherever possible make use of natural elements, not only for their fragrance but for their texture. Evergreens, dried and fresh flowers, pinecones, nuts, herbs, and fruit—gilded, crystallized, or au naturel—are your props, whether your taste runs to the plain or the fancy.

150 ❧ Decorating with Conifers

Use evergreen foliage generously throughout the house, in dried and fresh floral centerpieces; mantelpiece, banister, and window decorations; wreaths; and topiaries. Western hemlock, junipers, cypresses, silver firs, and pines are most successfully used, the latter three retain foliage especially well. Also make good use of the cones, either painted or natural, in your holiday decorating schemes. Before you start decorating, check your local florist, green market, nursery, or your own property for unusual plant materials to use in holiday decorations.

151 ⚡ Christmas Gilt

Gold, one of the gifts the wise men carried to Bethlehem, is a symbol of generosity. For a truly glittering Christmas, recycle miniature pumpkins and squash from Halloween and leftover fruit from Thanksgiving by spraying them with gold paint. Place them throughout the house or use them in arrangements, centerpieces, garlands, and topiaries. Gild walnuts and make ornaments out of them (see pages 49 and 96), also pinecones, bay leaves, dried flowers, lady apples, pomegranates, pineapples, lemons, and grapes. After spraying with gold paint, place on a raised rack overnight to dry. When using spray paints, work outdoors or if working indoors, be sure the room is well ventilated. Wear gloves, a dust mask, and glasses or goggles.

WREATHS AND OTHER WARM WELCOMES

A wreath is the symbol of welcome in the Christmas season. Hang one on your door or over the entryway mirror or fireplace. You can personalize a store-bought wreath or start from scratch and make your own.

152 ⚡ Potpourri Wreath

Green Styrofoam wreath
White glue
Potpourri
Glue gun

Pine and dried heather sprigs
2-inch-wide iridescent wire-edged
  ribbon

1. Coat the Styrofoam wreath section by section with glue and sprinkle with potpourri, covering the form completely. Let dry overnight.
2. Use a glue gun to attach a cluster of pine and heather sprigs to the bottom section of the wreath. Make a rosette and attach it.

153 ⚘ Braided Wreath for Birdies

PREP: 10 minutes   RISE: 30 minutes   COOK: 30 minutes
REST: 24 hours

When hung and allowed to dry outside, a bread wreath becomes both a decorative accent for your home and a winter feast for the birds. Wild bird food seeds are sold in many supermarkets and pet stores.

1 pound frozen white or wheat
*   bread dough, thawed*
1 egg

½ cup wild bird food seeds or
*   sesame seeds*

1. Grease outside of a 9-inch round cake pan and invert onto a greased baking sheet.

2. Roll out bread dough into a rope about 30 inches long. Using a sharp knife or kitchen shears, cut dough in half lengthwise and braid halves together. Wrap braided dough around cake pan on prepared baking sheet; pinch edges together to seal. Cover lightly with a kitchen towel and let rise in a warm place until almost doubled, about 30 minutes. Preheat oven to 375°F.

3. Bake wreath 20 minutes. In a small bowl, whisk egg until well blended. Brush generously over bread, cover with seeds, and bake 10 minutes longer, or until bread is nicely browned and bottom sounds hollow when tapped. Unmold and let dry, uncovered, on a rack for 24 hours. Decorate with a bow and hang on an exterior wall or door where birds will not be disturbed.

154 ⚘ Caliente Wreath

A chile-pepper wreath extends a particularly warm welcome. Buy an eighteen-inch wreath form and use florist wire to attach dried red chile peppers. Hang it or give it as a gift accompanied by a book on Southwestern cookery.

155 🎋 Vine Wreath

This wreath captures a bit of the joy of childhood.

Long pine sprigs
Florist wire
Grapevine wreath
Red and gold glass balls on wire
   (florist)

Glue gun
Pinecones
Miniature teddy bears
Wooden alphabet blocks
3-inch red velvet bow

   1. Attach sprigs of pine with florist wire to the lower half of a grapevine wreath, creating a fanlike effect. Wire in the glass balls, interspersing them throughout the pine.

   2. Use a glue gun to add pinecones, teddy bears, and blocks to spell out either "Noel" or "Joy." Wire a bow to the bottom of the wreath.

156 🎄 Candy Wreath

A candy wreath offers a sweet welcome, and when the holidays are over, it can be put away for next year or taken apart and eaten. The wreath is easy to make but it uses about 150 pieces of candy, so plan to do this with a friend. It's a good rainy-day project.

Wire hanger
Green and red curling ribbon
2½ pounds candy wrapped at both
  ends, such as flavored and filled
  sucking candies

3-inch-wide green or red velvet
  bow

1. Bend the hanger into a circle and the hook into a loop for hanging. Cut ribbon into 12-inch pieces, one for each piece of candy.
2. Curl the ribbon and tie each candy onto the hanger until the entire hanger is covered with the candy.
3. Finish with a bow tied to the top of the wreath.

157 🖋 Fragrant Wreath

The fresh fragrance of eucalyptus is unmistakable and its pale color sets the tone for a somewhat romantic wreath. Faded old milliner's flowers from the flea market are perfect, but new will do nicely too.

Florist wire
Pale pink or lavender fabric roses
Eucalyptus wreath
Glue
Dried baby's breath

2-inch-wide silk ribbon, to match roses
¼-inch-wide silk ribbon, to match roses
Raffia to match roses

　　1. Wire fabric roses into the wreath and glue bits of baby's breath to the flowers.
　　2. Make a large rosette bow with wide ribbon and then glue streamers of narrow ribbon and raffia to the bow. Wire the bow to the wreath.

158 🖋 Long Lasting Wreath

This wreath makes good seasonal use of the echeveria plant's dense rosettes. Best of all, it lasts long after the holidays are over.

14-inch wreath frame
Peat moss

Echeveria plants
Floral picks

　　Cover the wreath frame with peat moss. Take the plants out of their pots and insert the roots into the moss and anchor them with floral picks. Water as you would any houseplant.

159 🌿 Traditional Williamsburg Welcome

In historic Williamsburg, Virginia, where Christmas is celebrated as it was in the 1770s, magnolia leaves, boxwood, citrus
fruit, and apples are the traditional ingredients in the *demi-lune*
sprays over the front doors. A pineapple, the colonial symbol of
welcome, goes on top. The greens are gathered from the woods
surrounding the town.

Plywood
Green paint
Seven-penny finishing nails
Boxwood and pine sprigs
Apples, oranges, limes, and
   lemons

Florist wire
1 pineapple
Basic Garland (see page 94)

1. Measure the width of your front doorway, cut a piece of
plywood in a semicircle to that width, and paint it green. With a
pencil score concentric circles onto the piece of wood. Every 2
inches on each line drive in a finishing nail halfway. Staple the
boxwood and pine onto the plywood.

2. Pierce each piece of fruit with florist wire and attach the
fruit to the nails, alternating rows of apples, oranges, limes, and
lemons. Place a pineapple at the very top of the doorway. Add a
garland on each side of the doorway and attach more fruit with
florist wire at 6-inch intervals.

160 🍁 Handy Wreath

What could be more welcoming than an outstretched hand? This paper wreath is fun for kids to make and hang on the door to their room.

Trace the hands of each person in the family. Place the tracings on the top sheet of several layers of gift wrap or origami paper and carefully cut through all the layers along the tracing. Glue each of the hands onto a cardboard wreath with fingers facing out from the center until it is completely covered. When the glue dries, use a pencil to roll the fingers toward the palm of each hand, then do the same with the thumbs. Fluff the paper out and attach a wire or ribbon loop for hanging.

161 🍁 Luminarias

Luminarias are traditional in the southwestern part of the country where they are used on garden paths, patios, and front porches. A row of luminarias lights up the approach to your home.

Use small white bakery bags and create a design on them with a hole punch or use them plain. Put sand, gravel, coarse salt, or kitty litter in the bottom of the bag and firmly anchor a votive candle inside. For added safety use glass holders for the candles.

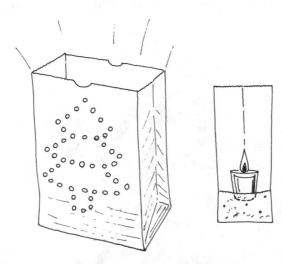

Versatile rope garlands of evergreens can be dressed up or down for use in a variety of ways. Hang one over the doorway to your home or the entrance to your living room, use one as a swag over the mantelpiece or around the windows, entwine one around fence railings and lampposts outside and banisters inside. You can buy lengths of garland from the florist or tree seller and create your own by using a basic garland and the variations that follow. When hanging garland, use medium gauge wire and finishing nails gently hammered in where the holes will be least likely to show.

162 ❧ Seasonal Centerpieces

Make your dinner table center stage with a festive evergreen garland centerpiece that sets the style for your holiday dinner or buffet table.

163 ❧ Basic Garland

With florist wire, attach bunches of holly, boxwood, and white pine to a six-foot length of thick rope, twisting them onto the rope so it is no longer visible. Embellish using one of the following variations.

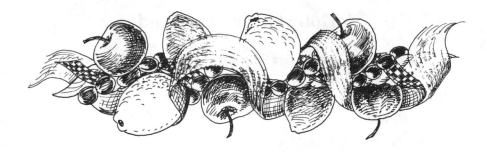

164   Traditional Colonial Garland

The colonial garland gives a traditional country look when used on the table or over the fireplace. Use the fruit au naturel.

Crab apples, lemons, and limes   *Cranberries*
Basic Garland   *½-inch-wide plaid ribbon*
Florist wire

    Attach crab apples, lemons, and limes to the garland with florist wire. Thread clusters of cranberries on wire and attach them to the garland. Weave ribbon around the garland.

165   Country Garland

The country garland makes a delightful centerpiece. It also looks pretty hanging over an interior doorway or swagged over the mantelpiece or windows.

Dried flowers, such as hydrangeas,   *Cinnamon sticks*
*   roses, heather, and baby's*   *Nuts*
*   breath*   *½-inch-wide ribbon, color coordi-*
Basic Garland   *nated to table setting*
Florist wire

    Attach small bunches of dried flowers to the garland with florist wire. Add clusters of cinnamon sticks and nuts. Entwine a ribbon through the garland.

166 ⚘ Glorious Gilded Garland

A gilded garland makes a dazzling centerpiece.

Basic Garland   *Florist wire*
Gold spray paint   *½-inch-wide gold ribbon*
Pineapple, grapes, lemons, nuts

Spray-paint fruits and nuts and wire them into the garland. Wind gold ribbon loosely around the entire length of the garland.

167 ⚘ Crystallized Fruit Bowl

Create a beautiful still-life centerpiece of sugar-glazed fruit. For the most interest choose a variety of shapes, colors, and sizes of fruit; use lady apples, pears, small clusters of grapes, plums, nectarines, cherries, and lemons. Dip each piece of fruit into egg white, allow the excess to drip off. Cover a large plate with superfine granulated sugar and gently roll each piece in the sugar until it is completely covered. Place the fruit on aluminum foil to dry. Choose a pretty bowl for display. If you intend to use the fruit in a wreath or garland, thread a thin piece of wire through the fruit before coating with egg white. Note: Because of the threat of salmonella from raw eggs these should not be eaten.

168 ❦ Winter Wonderland Centerpiece

This centerpiece is very dramatic, especially when the room lights are turned out. For a less stark image, set some low bud vases holding small bunches of white flowers—roses, paper-whites, and Thai orchids among others—at the edges. Finish by setting tea lights in and around the centerpiece.

White Styrofoam,
   3 feet X 2 inches X 8 inches
Double-sided tape
White birch branches,
   12 to 18 inches

White Christmas lights with
   white cords, with a battery pack
   if possible
Spray fixative
Iridescent snow confetti

1. Tape the Styrofoam to the table with double-sided tape so that it is secure. Stick branches into the Styrofoam to create a forest effect. Lay the lights down along the Styrofoam so that you can see how to distribute them evenly. With the lights on, work them into the branches.

2. Spray the branches with fixative and sprinkle snow confetti over them. Use additional confetti to cover any trace of the Styrofoam base.

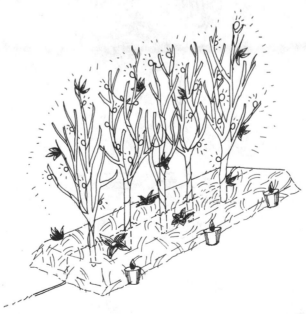

169  Traditional Williamsburg Topiary

Topiaries are miniature trees for the table. Pyramid or round, single or double, small or tall, with dried flowers, fruit, nuts, or pinecones, they make very special seasonal centerpieces.

Medium clay pot   *Berries and nuts, in the shell*
Marble chips   *Sheet moss*
18-inch birch branch   *Gold or silver cord*
6-inch Styrofoam ball   *Gold or silver streamer ribbons*
Glue gun

1. Fill the pot with marble chips. Stick the branch into the Styrofoam ball. Using a hot-glue gun, attach berries and nuts to the ball, filling in any spaces with moss.

2. Wrap gold or silver cord around the ball and set it in the pot. Tie streamer ribbons around the bottom of the stem.

170 🕯 Candled Apples

13 large yellow apples
13 tea lights or votive candles
Lemon juice
Footed cake plate

Boxwood leaves
Lemons or limes
Thick toothpicks

1. Cut the bottom off the apples so they stay in place without rolling. Place a tea light on top of each apple and with a knife, score a circle around the candle. Cut down and scoop out enough of the apple so that all of the candle is below the rim. Sprinkle lemon juice on the apple to prevent it from browning.

2. Cover the cake plate with boxwood leaves and place 5 apples in an evenly spaced circle. Fill the middle of the circle with lemons or limes. Stick toothpicks into the bottom of 4 of the remaining apples and place them on top of the lemons or limes, securing them with toothpicks. Repeat with 3 more apples, and then with the last one to make a pyramid.

171 🕯 Edible Centerpieces & Favors

Use these as centerpieces to be passed around or to pick from when the meal is over.

- Cookie Tree (see page 125)
- Croquembouche (see page 180)
- Bûche de Noël (see page 204)

172 🕯 Popcorn Christmas Trees

These little trees, made with icing and sugar ice-cream cones, are fun for a children's table. Make a "forest" centerpiece or place one at each setting.

Use the recipe on page 189 to make a smooth icing, adding a few drops of food coloring to tint it light green. Spread over the outside of the cones, using about two tablespoons to cover completely. Before the icing hardens, press popped corn all over the cone. Use red M&M's or red–hots for ornaments and sprinkle with green colored sugar.

173   Tray Chic

Look for ice trays that form ice in the shape of hearts, stars, and trees instead of cubes. Fill the stars or hearts with cranberry juice. For the trees, add a little green food coloring to water. Set them out on the table in a clear ice bowl to serve with club soda.

174   Potpourri Balls

Sometimes potpourri gets so old it loses its scent. Use some to make these Christmas balls to place in a bowl or hang on your tree.

3-inch Styrofoam balls   *¼-inch-wide ribbon*
White glue   *Straight pins*
Potpourri that has lost its scent

 1. Coat the Styrofoam ball with glue. Roll the ball in potpourri and let dry.

 2. Lay out 3 pieces of ribbon so they intersect in the middle. Place ball where ribbons cross. Tack the ribbon into the sides of the ball with straight pins and then tie at the top into a bow.

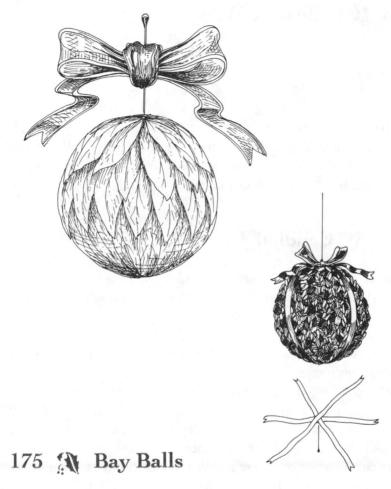

175 🌿 Bay Balls

You'll need a lot of bay leaves to make these aromatic balls. If you prefer, cover the Styrofoam ball with velvet florist's leaves and use pearl-topped corsage pins for little berries. Place several balls in an urn or on a decorative platter or hang them on the tree.

Fresh bay leaves
3-inch Styrofoam balls
Hot-glue gun

1-inch-wide gold wire ribbon
Hat pins

Working slowly, apply each leaf to the Styrofoam ball with a hot-glue gun in an overlapping fashion. Tie a piece of ribbon into a bow and secure it to the ball with a hat pin.

176 🐦 Pinecone Balls

Sheet moss
Styrofoam balls
Glue gun

Miniature pinecones
Berries
Silk tassel

Moisten moss to make it pliable and glue it to the Styrofoam ball with the glue gun. Attach pinecones until the ball is completely covered. Add berries for color and finish with a tassel hanging from the bottom of the ball.

177 🐦 Candlelight

Candles ensure the warmth of Christmas, so light your room only with their glow. Just make sure there is enough light wherever your guests will sit or stand.

- Place a holiday candle at each place setting, tying ribbon or fabric around glass votive holders.
- Set baskets filled with glass votive candles around the room.
- Core several fresh artichokes and allow them to dry out. Spray with gold paint and let dry overnight. Insert a votive candle in each and use on the table or mantel.
- Set out an array of different-colored candles in candlesticks of varying heights in front of a large mirror, doubling the effect. Place glass votives on shelves in front of small mirrors to reflect the glow.
- Use magnolia or lemon leaves at the base of tall candles; it's an attractive way to catch dripping wax.
- Freeze holiday candles and they will burn slower.
- Remember that beeswax candles don't drip at all.
- Always reuse partially burned candles.
- Mass a colored assortment of fat dripless candles on one or two cookie trays or mirror squares disguised with sprigs of holly or boxwood.

CHRISTMAS SCENTS

The tree and other greens, pomanders, potpourri, cinnamon sticks, masses of paperwhites, sugar and spice aromas from the kitchen, these are the fragrances of the season.

178 ❦ Pomander Balls

A pomander is a lime, lemon, or orange covered with whole cloves. Pomanders can be given as gifts to be used year-round in closets and drawers or displayed in a bowl. They can also be hung on a tree or included in a potpourri.

Stick a pushpin into the fruit, remove, and insert a clove. In the traditional pomander, cloves are placed so close to one another that the heads touch and the whole fruit is covered. If you want the pomanders to stay fragrant for years, place it in a paper bag containing powdered orris root, seal the bag, and shake. Store the bag in a warm dark spot for 3 weeks. Tie a velvet, lace, or gold ribbon around the pomander for hanging.

179 ❦ Display Pomanders

If the pomanders are to be used solely for display, stud the fruit in patterns. Draw diamonds, loops, or a checkerboard, then use the cloves in single rows or fill areas of the design solidly with them. Arrange these in a pyramid as a centerpiece or add a few to a garland.

180 ❦ Potpourri

Potpourri, literally "rotted pot," was originally formed by layering dead plant material and aromatic gums and salts in a pot and allowing them to ferment. The fragrant though not very pretty results were then put into a decorative container and warmed by the fire to bring out the fragrance. Common potpourri ingredients are cinnamon sticks, orange peel, dried flowers, and tree cones (see page 107). Use potpourri in all your rooms but be sure to place a large beautiful basket or bowl of it on a table in the entryway to greet guests with fragrance.

181 ❦ More Seasonal Fragrance

• Place orange rinds, cinnamon sticks, cloves, and fresh ginger in a saucepan, cover with water, and bring to a boil. Simmer on low heat.
• Combine an ounce of cinnamon sticks, an ounce and a half of whole cloves, half an ounce of fresh or dried bay leaves, and an ounce of ground allspice in a saucepan, stir, and simmer for two minutes. Set out in a decorative bowl.
• Warm the oven, turn it off, then sprinkle cinnamon on a cookie sheet and put it in the oven.
• Throw orange rinds and pinecones into the fireplace.
• Use fragrant woods for burning.
• Use fragrant firestarters (see page 50).

HOLIDAY TABLE FAVORS

These are colorful decorative accents that your guests get to take home with them.

182 ❦ Scented Sentiments Favor

A party favor for each guest to take home and light on Christmas Eve. Put one at each place setting or arrange in a basket near the door to give to guests as they leave.

3- X 5-inch blank card stock tags *Red, green, or gold tissue paper*
Bayberry-scented votive candle in *Curling ribbon*
  a glass holder

1. Write the following saying onto each tag or have a rubber stamp made and use that.

On Christmas Eve
A Bayberry Candle
Burned to the Socket
Brings Good Luck
To the House
And Money to the Pocket

2. Wrap each candle like a party cracker in a 4- X 8-inch piece of tissue paper, gathering, pinching, and twisting the paper about 2 inches in at both ends. Tie at each pinched point with several pieces of ribbon in different lengths. Curl the ribbon with scissors. Attach the tag to one of the pieces of ribbon.

183 ❦ Doing a Favor

For a special environmentally aware party favor that will last long after Christmas, put a little cedar tree ready for planting at each place setting.

184 ⚑ Buy Crackers

From Victorian England comes the tradition of crackers containing toys, jokes, and paper crowns. Order them from the Smithsonian Institution (eleven to a box) and use them as party favors at Christmas dinner.

185 ⚑ Surprise Rolls

Make your own Christmas crackers for the kids, using cardboard tubes from wrapping paper, paper towels, wax paper, aluminum foil, and toilet tissue. Cut the tubes into pieces about three and a half inches long. Take a ten- by twenty-inch piece of red or green crepe paper and create ruffles on the long side by grasping the paper between thumb and forefinger at one-inch intervals and stretching it. Center the cardboard tube on the paper and roll it up, pinching the paper together at one end and tying it with a long piece of curling ribbon. Fill the tube with candies, popcorn, and any other tiny treats you can find. Pinch the other end together and tie with a second piece of curling ribbon. Open out the ruffled ends to look like a flower, then curl the ribbon streamers; add more ribbon if desired. Decorate with Christmas stickers, rubber-stamped images, or glue and glitter. These may also be hung on the tree.

186   Sachet Away

Give sweetly fragrant sachets as party favors. You can make your own potpourri sachets using this recipe. You should have enough for six sachets. They also make fragrant party favors.

4 cups red rosebuds and petals
3 or 4 lemon leaves
3 or 4 sprigs tallow berries
2 pomanders made of crab or lady
   apples
2 pinecones
½ cup oak moss
30 drops rose oil
30 drops cinnamon oil

30 drops bergamot oil
2 cups cinnamon sticks cut into
   1-inch pieces
6 pieces festive fabric,
   8 X 18 inches each
6 lengths silk wire ribbon,
   18 inches long
Pinecones, holly sprigs with
   berries, fabric roses

1. Mix all the ingredients except the fabric together. Fill a bowl with the mixture and let stand in a cool dry place for at least 1 week; shake occasionally.

2. Fold a piece of fabric in two and stitch one side and the top. Pink the other side and leave it open. Fill the sack with the potpourri, gather the fabric at the opening, and tie with a piece of ribbon. Glue some pinecones, sprigs of holly berries, and a fabric rose at the center of the bow.

187   Heart-shape Sachets

This gift makes good use of old silk ties to make heart-shape sachets. Carefully remove the thread from the underside of the tie and open it flat, keeping the pouch created by the lining intact. Iron the tie flat. With the tie open and reverse side up, cut the wide end of the tie five inches above the end of the lining and hem. Fill the lining pouch with potpourri, fold the cut side of the tie over, and insert it at least one inch into the pouch of potpourri, tucking in the center to create the heart shape. Close the sachet by tying a silk ribbon around the pouch.

188   Dual Favor

For a place card and favor to take and hang on the tree, spell out the guest's name in silver glitter on a large gold Christmas ball.

189   Napkins That Ring

Make seasonal napkin rings for guests to take home with them and hang on their tree. String little jingle bells on wire (use an empty paper towel roll as a form), then tie a red bow on each.

TABLE MANNERS

190   Starry, Starry Night

Make stars your party decor theme. Use a star cookie cutter to shape butter patties for the table. Use trays that make ice in star shapes, adding red or green food coloring to the water, and place in a glass ice bucket. Strew little silver stars on the table.

191   For a Victorian Dinner

• Follow the Victorian custom of having an ornate place card at each setting that can be hung on the tree after dinner.
• Cover a little box with a gold doily and fill with ribbon candy, a Victorian favorite.
• Use an antique lace tablecloth and tie the napkins with crimson or gold ribbon and tiny sprigs of greenery.
• Attach a bow holding some fragrant greens at each of the corners of the tablecloth.
• Tie a wide ribbon around the chair back and finish with a huge bow at the back.

192 🎄 M&M's the Word

Make individual Christmas tree party favors for each of the kids using sugar ice cream cones covered with icing (see page 189) onto which you stick M&M's as ornaments. To carry the theme further, scatter M&M's over the table in a random fashion. Use a red tablecloth and napkins that match the colors of the M&M's.

193 🎄 Dessert Buffet

Arrange cookies and cakes on the dessert buffet in interesting containers. Use small floral hatboxes, old wooden cigar boxes, antique and reproduction tins, and low woven baskets and serving trays. Line them first with gold or other color tissue paper, leaving the ends loose to frame the edibles.

194 🎄 Quick & Easy Holiday Decorations

You needn't spend a great deal of time, money, and effort on seasonal decorations.

- Lay sprays of evergreens on the mantelpiece, thread a string of white lights (on green wire) through them, and nestle some of your collectibles amid the greens.
- Fold a fringed shawl into a triangle, drape it on the mantel with the fringe dipping over the edge, and create a still life of candelabrum, bibelots, and dried flowers on top.
- Place several different sizes of poinsettia plants in cachepots or baskets and add trailing ivy.
- Cover the mantel or a wide windowsill with a bed of Spanish moss, tuck in pieces of ivy and holly, pinecones, natural or painted, and a few gilded nuts and fruit (see pages 49 and 87).
- Fill cachepots, terra-cotta pots, or baskets with pinecones and place on the mantel or windowsills.

- Set out a bowl of lady apples and pomanders on a bed of evergreen in the living room.
- Use wooden bowls, baskets, and stoneware and ceramic pitchers and cachepots for a country or rustic look.
- Use silver, porcelain, and china holders for a more formal look.
- Festoon gates, railings, and lampposts with garlands of greens dotted with pinecones and holly; add strings of white lights.
- Drape a long rope of greens over the front door, letting it fall halfway to the ground on each side; attach a red velvet or satin bow over the doorway, and encircle the garland with a streamer of the same ribbon. Frame the entry further by placing a full red poinsettia plant on each side of the doorway.
- Hang your holiday wreath with a four-inch-wide silk ribbon right onto a mirror in the entryway or over the mantelpiece.
- Decorate the rim of a hanging basket by gluing on Spanish moss, clusters of colorful straw flowers, dried statice, and heather and fill it with fresh apples.
- Fill a woven basket with large pinecones interspersed with clusters of delicate baby's breath, then thread tiny white lights throughout, hiding the wires under the pinecones.
- Tie an iridescent wire-edged ribbon around a basket holding fruit, finishing with a festive bow.
- Place extra mirrors around the house during the holidays to add to the glow by reflecting and multiplying the special effects of your decorations.
- Wind strands of tiny white Christmas lights and greens around and up the banister; tie large plaid ribbons along the way.
- Place a poinsettia or flowering plant on every step, to peek through the banister.
- Hang flat snowflake ornaments on the firescreen to create an interesting illusion against the warming blaze.
- Place an arrangement of boxwood, dried flowers, berries, and crystallized fruit (see page 96) in a rectangular woven basket wrapped with wire-edged ribbon, on the entry table.
- Use a galvanized pail for an ice bucket and tie a big calico bow or two western-style bandannas around it for a casual country look for a party.

- Fill a small burlap bag with sand, marble chips, or kitty litter, roll down the top, and place on an entry table or mantel. Stuff with sprigs of pine and berried holly and fresh apples and pears; sticking in one or two dripless taper candles.
- Tape, tie, or staple Christmas cards to ribbon streamers to hang for display.

DECORATE WITH SEASONAL FLOWERS

Seasonal plants and flowers fill the house with beauty and color, and some with fragrance as well. They represent easy and relatively inexpensive decorative touches, especially when placed in eye-catching containers. All are available from nurseries and florist shops; several may be easily forced from bulbs. Plants to brighten your holiday season besides those described here include freesia, jasmine, star of Bethlehem, crown of thorns, and the Aztec lily.

195   The Reliable Poinsettia

By the end of the nineteenth century this native Mexican and Central American shrub *(Euphorbia pulcherrima)* with its clusters of bright red bracts became one of this country's most popular Christmas decorations. Starting in the 1920s skillful breeding led to longer lasting, larger poinsettias in white, cream, and pale rose in addition to the ever popular Christmas red.

To maintain your poinsettias' beauty through the holiday season, keep them well watered; in bright but not hot light during the day, cool (60°F or lower) at night; and out of drafts, day and night. Plants will start to fade naturally in January or February.

When this happens, cut off the stalks, leaving just three joints at the base of each stem. For the next six weeks keep the plant dry and cool, then start to water. The moment new shoots appear, fertilize with an all-purpose fertilizer. With the onset of warmer weather, set the plant outdoors in a sunny but sheltered spot, either sinking the pot into the ground up to its rim or putting the plant directly into the ground. Early in July pinch back each new shoot to one or two joints and keep the plant well watered and fed throughout the summer. In late September take the plant indoors and place it where it will get bright light, but no more than 10 hours a day. Move to a cool, dark place, a cellar or closet, every night. At this point, poinsettias need at least fourteen hours of complete darkness each night. When the color of the plant is well developed bring it out for display and normal care.

196 🎄 More Christmas Plants

- *Amaryllis:* The amaryllis (*Hippeastrum vittatum*) is often referred to as the "Christmas lily." Its flowers have come to symbolize a trumpet heralding the birth of Jesus. It is easily grown from bulbs (see page 19).
- *Christmas cactus:* This cactus (*Schlumbergera truncata*) is a tropical plant which blossoms at yuletide with striking red bells.
- *Holly:* The red berries of holly (*Ilex aquifolium*) have come to symbolize the arrival of Christ on earth.
- *Leaf plant:* Because the leaf plant (*Kalanchoe blossfeldiana*) produces new growth at Christmastime, it has come to symbolize redemption.
- *Paperwhites:* The fragrant paperwhite narcissus (*Narcissus tazetta*), with its dainty fragrant blossoms, is the easiest flowering bulb to force (see page 18).

197 🐿 A Glimpse of Stockings

In the 1820s and 1830s Christmas stockings were made by the children of the family. Needless to say they were generously proportioned to hold that much more. By Victorian times stockings had become elaborately embellished. To make a nostalgic stocking look in flea markets and antique shops for a quilt remnant made up of country calicos and small prints; for an elegant stocking, look for a piece of silk-and-velvet Victorian crazy quilt.

Enlarge the pattern on page 263 to scale. Place the pattern on the wrong side of the quilt remnant and trace with a marker. Cut an 18- X 22-inch rectangle of muslin and another of cotton batting. Baste the wrong side of the quilt piece to batting. Use your sewing machine to quilt-stitch through all of the thicknesses. Trim excess fabric, leaving seam allowances. Use the pattern to cut another stocking shape out of the quilt remnant. Put together with the quilted stocking piece, right sides facing, and stitch along the edges, leaving the top edge open. Finish the edges and turn to right side. Cut a cuff of the quilt remnant to fit the upper edge. Sew short ends of the cuff together to form a circular shape. Pin the right side of the cuff to the wrong side of the stocking aligning the raw edges. Sew together, finish the edges and turn the cuff to the right side. Add a loop of grosgrain ribbon to a country quilt stocking, one of velvet or lace to a Victorian quilt stocking for hanging.

PART FOUR

The Tree

CHAPTER 7

To Tree or Not to Tree

The Christmas tree as we know it first
appeared in Germany in the seventeenth
century. Apples, wafers, and sweets were
among the first decorations, which led
to the name "sugar tree."
It is thought that Hessian soldiers fighting in
the American Revolutionary War brought
with them their Christmas custom of
decorating an evergreen. Less than a century
later, the first commercial ornaments to be
sold here were handblown glass balls and
icicles made in Germany.
As the tradition developed in this country, the
type of tree used and how it was decorated
varied from region to region. In places where
there were no native evergreens, imagination
and ingenuity found substitutes—like
decorated tumbleweeds in the prairie states.
President Theodore Roosevelt, worried about
the depletion of the national forests, for a time
banned a cut tree from the White House.
Today most trees destined for holiday use are
raised on farms, and the Christmas tree
industry has become the largest planter of new
trees in the nation.

198 🎄 Buying a Cut Tree

Determine the size and type of tree you want before going shopping. Also know where in the house it will stand. If it's to be placed in a corner, for example, it need not be perfectly shaped all around. Measure the height of the room, and remember to allow for the height of the tree stand.

199 🎄 Types of Christmas Trees

Fourteen types of evergreens are sold in the United States for use as Christmas trees: balsam fir, Douglas fir, white fir, grand fir, Scotch pine, red pine, Austrian pine, Virginia pine, white pine, Eastern red cedar, blue spruce, red spruce, black spruce, and Norway spruce. The most popular are the Douglas fir, balsam fir, and Scotch pine. The firs are the most fragrant.

Fir and Scotch pine are the longest-lasting trees, a good choice if you like to put the tree up early and take it down after New Year's. Scotch pine is particularly popular because even if it's neglected it doesn't drop its needles. The thick branches of blue spruce lend themselves to elaborate decorations, but spruce is the quickest tree to dry out.

200 🎄 Fresh Test

To test for freshness, bounce the tree: If it's fresh, only a few needles will fall. (Don't try this with spruce, which normally doesn't retain needles well.) Pull at the needles at the top of a branch: If they pull off easily, the tree is already dry and won't last long in a heated room. Needles should offer resistance to pulling and be resilient if bent. Inquire whether the tree has been dyed to look fresher than it is. Check for yourself by looking at the underside of the needles—if it has been dyed you will see a difference in color.

201 ✒ Putting the Tree Up

Until you are ready to put the tree up, keep it outdoors in a cool shaded spot sheltered from wind or indoors in an unheated room. When you are ready to put it up, saw one inch off the bottom of the trunk, preferably on a slant. Place fresh boiling water in the tree stand (one with a generous reservoir) to melt the sap; and replenish as the level goes down. Never let the water go below the bottom of the trunk. Avoid placing the tree near anything that gives off heat, like a fireplace or television set.

202 ✒ Taking the Tree Down

Recycle all or some of the tree. Use the branches as mulch; place them on empty window boxes, outdoor planters, or in city tree pits. Nearly all cities have Christmas tree recycling programs where wood chipping machines turn discarded cut trees into mulch. Find out the location of one near you. When you take the tree down:

- Wind strings of lights onto empty paper towel rolls to eliminate having to unravel knots next year.
- Pack ornaments away using empty egg cartons, discarded wrapping paper, and tissue paper.
- Put garlands of popcorn on the trees outside for the birds.

203 ✒ Fancy Plants

Instead of buying a cut or living tree just for the holidays, bedeck your large houseplants for the season. Tie a very wide festive ribbon around the rim of the pot and finish with a large bow or wrap the pot in red and green plaid taffeta or red velvet. String tiny white lights through larger plants or hang them with miniature candy canes. Ficus, schefflera, dracaena, and Norfolk pine are among the houseplants that lend themselves to decorating.

204 🐦 A Living Tree

Instead of a cut tree, consider buying a live evergreen tree from a nursery or garden center to be planted after Christmas. It must not, however, dry out. When you get it home, let the ball soak up water, then remove the burlap covering the roots and allow excess water to drain. Wrap the root ball in plastic and tie with cord to secure. Buy an antidesiccant from the nursery and spray the branches; this allows the passage of oxygen and carbon dioxide but prevents loss of moisture. Avoid setting the tree too near a heat source like a radiator. *Don't keep your living tree indoors for more than a week.* If after Christmas the ground is frozen, store the tree outdoors in a sheltered unheated space with the root ball covered with a blanket.

205 🐦 Trees in Situ

Drape waterproof red ribbon all around or cascading down maypole-style from the top of small trees on your patio or lawn. Add bows of the same material if you wish.

206 🐦 A Hanging Tree

Hang this tree on the wall with a table in front of it to hold the presents. Nail together a wooden triangle the size you want. Wrap chicken wire around it, then completely cover the chicken wire sheet with moss. Using a glue gun, attach dried white statice to the moss. Wire a piece of bark to the bottom for a trunk. If you wish, add some small gold and red balls.

207 🐦 Twiggy

Creating a holiday focal point without buying a tree is as simple as gathering an armful of bare branches approximately six feet long, setting them in a silver wine cooler, and bringing them to life with a string of white lights.

208 🕯 Ersatz Christmas Tree

This faux tree is very stylish indeed.

Chicken wire, 4 feet × 45 inches
Tall birch branch,
   5 feet × 3 inches
2 pieces of ¼-inch wood,
   18 inches long
Florist wire

12-inch terra-cotta pot, preferably
   aged (see page 19)
Marble chips
Sheet moss
Pine sprigs
Christmas lights and ornaments

1. Form the chicken wire into a cone 4 feet high and 18 inches in diameter at the bottom. Stick the cone over the top of the branch. To secure the cone in place, take 2 pieces of wood and attach to the bottom of the cone on either side of the tree branch with wire.

2. Stick the "tree" into the pot and anchor it with marble chips. Push pieces of sheet moss along with pine sprigs into the chicken wire until you can no longer see it. Add lights and ornaments to taste.

209 🐿 The Ladder Tree

Place a six-foot wooden stepladder in a corner of the room in such a way that the back of it is not visible. Tack long and short evergreen branches to the front and sides of the ladder; wire the smallest sprigs to the rungs. Fill in so that all of the ladder is covered with greens, then decorate as you would any tree; use the rungs to hold toys, teddy bears, tiny books, alphabet blocks, and any other old-fashioned collectibles you may have. At the top place an angel or a star, or something as unorthodox as your "tree," like a pinwheel.

Another ladder tree that really fools the eye takes just three large and very full branches, the same height as the ladder. Attach one with wire to the front of the ladder "growing" up, and the two others to either side "growing" down.

210   Container Trees

Potted and clipped trees, such as boxwood, bay, yew, and privet, may be brought indoors from the garden or terrace, decorated for Christmas with tiny white lights and small ornaments, and then put back out when the holiday is over.

211   Holly Bush

18-inch terra-cotta pot, aged (see page 19)
Plaster of Paris
Birch branch, 3½ feet long
Sheet moss
Green Styrofoam ball, 10 inches in diameter

About 30 holly sprigs, with berries
Tiny white lights
Iridescent wire-edged ribbon

    1. Fill the pot with plaster of Paris and anchor the branch in the wet mix. Let dry.

    2. Cover plaster of Paris with moss. Center the Styrofoam ball on the branch and gently press down to attach. Stick the holly sprigs into the Styrofoam. Weave the lights through the holly and tie a bow around the trunk.

212   Poinsettia Tree

Place poinsettia plants wrapped in red foil on every rung of a small wooden stepladder. Start the first row on the floor in a semicircle around the base of the ladder. Alternate rows of pale plants with deep red ones. The plants should be very full. If you have a pyramid plant stand, use that instead of the ladder.

213 ✿ Tabletop Trees

In the early nineteenth century, holiday trees were small enough to set on tabletops. Some homes boasted of several trees, a large one in the parlor and several diminutive but lavishly decorated trees in halls, on the stairs, and in other rooms. The tradition of the tabletop tree, said to have been started by Queen Victoria and Prince Albert, is perfect for a small city apartment. But don't underestimate the dramatic value of a petite tree, no matter where you live. This size tree with a root ball is easy to use for landscaping purposes.

214 ✿ Love & Kisses Tree

Make your tree an ode to romance. Use a string of little pink lights; make paper garlands of hearts cut from red foil paper; fill tiny red baskets with silver, red, and green foil-wrapped candy kisses; hang silver foil hearts, red satin hearts, puffy plaid fabric hearts, and any other hearts you had the forethought to save from Valentine's Day. Look for pictures of ruby-red lips featured in lipstick ads, cut them out, and mount on small heart-shape and round doilies. Get a rubber stamp of lips and a red ink pad and stamp some of the heart-shape ornaments. Add a few little teddy bears—for bear hugs, of course. For more ideas, see the paper and lace heart ornaments on pages 56 and 132.

215 ✿ Baby's First Tree

String a tree with tiny white lights, then tie the following onto the branches, using blue or pink ribbons. Rattles, small stuffed toys, the first comb and brush, teething rings, booties, and miniature frames holding pictures of the family's newest member. Buy one ornament especially for this tree. Each year continue the tradition of buying a special ornament for this child and others to come. When they're older, the children can place their ornaments themselves; when they're grown and out on their own, they'll have a starter set of decorations.

216 🕭 The Cookie Tree

This tree makes a wonderful centerpiece for a children's party. If the kids are old enough, make the baking, decorating, and trimming all part of the party fun. Use the cookie recipe (see page 188) to make a batch of cookies cut into shapes of stars, hearts, Santas, trees, and farm animals. Remember before baking to make a hole for hanging. Use a basic icing (see page 189) to decorate the cookies, then spread thin plaid or gingham ribbon through the holes and hang the cookies from the branches of the tree.

217 🕭 A Fragrant Herb Tree

For a delightful holiday accent for a country kitchen, place the tree in a woven basket and trim it with small ribbon-tied clusters of fresh sage, pennyroyal, oregano, lavender, mountain mint, and cinnamon sticks. Add little bunches of dried flowers like statice and star of Bethlehem. When Christmas is over recycle the herbs and spices by using them as seasonings and for making potpourri.

218 🕭 Miniature Trees as Gifts

Miniature potted evergreens make thoughtful gifts when decorated to reflect the interest of the person to whom it is being given. If you give one without decorations either place it in a woven basket or cover the burlap root ball with a piece of velvet or gingham fabric and tie with a festive ribbon.

- *For the gardener on your list:* Decorate a small fir tree with trowel, gardening gloves, packets of seeds, bulbs, and a couple of small herb plants.
- *For the needlecrafts person on your list:* Decorate with a colorful selection of skeins of embroidery floss, a small embroidery hoop, thimbles, packets of needles, and pincushions; attach small bows of lace trim and a pair of sewing scissors.

- *For the baker on your list:* Decorate with new or vintage cookie cutters and small chocolate molds and such practical devices as a candy thermometer; place the tree in an oversized baking mitt.

. . . AND ALL THE TRIMMINGS

Prominent among early handmade ornaments were handblown glass balls, wax cherubs with spun-glass wings, and light-catching concave reflectors. Kugels, popular in the 1850s, were lead-lined glass balls filled with colored wax. These were used to weigh down boughs holding candles in order to avoid setting fire to the branches above. Just before World War II, Corning Glass was convinced by the German ornament maker Max Eckhardt that the glass balls could be manufactured by adapting the machines that turned out electric light bulbs. In many families such early ornaments have been handed down through the generations. In recent years they have become highly prized (and highly priced) collectibles for sale year-round at antique shops and flea markets.

219 🍇 Trimming the Tree

Dry resinous trees are highly flammable. Before you start to trim, examine all strings of lights for breaks or frays; when in doubt, discard. Try to place nonflammable decorations closest to the lights and *never* use candles. *Always* unplug the lights when you go out, even if it's for a short time. When you buy new lights, test them in the store; it will save time and tempers if they are defective. For outside the house, use only lights and cords labeled for outdoor use.

Children, puppies, and especially cats have a fascination for extension cords and how they taste. Chewing on them could cause shock or a burn. With that in mind, before you string the lights on the tree dab the cord with chile pepper sauce and let it dry.

220 ✒ The Nitty Gritty of Trimming

Some people like to cover their trees with so many ornaments and tinsel that the branches are completely obscured; others, the minimalists, want the natural beauty of the tree to be the focus of attention. For the rest of us here is a way to calculate a middle-of-the-road approach:

2-foot tree = 10 feet of garland; 25 to 35 ornaments
4-foot tree = 40 feet of garland; 50 to 75 ornaments
6-foot tree = 75 feet of garland; 100 to 150 ornaments
7½-foot tree = 100 feet of garland; 175 to 275 ornaments

Lights go on first, garlands next, then the ornaments. How many lights? If you are using tiny lights, multiply the width of the tree in feet by eight times its height. If you plan to use larger lights, multiply the tree's width in feet by three times the height. It's a matter of tradition in each household as to whether the star or angel or other tree topper is the first or last item placed on the tree. Of course it's easier to attach it first but more dramatic not to mention challenging to save it for last.

221 ✒ Tiny Trimmers

If small children are involved in the trimming and want to place the ornaments themselves, allow them to go first. Never leave Christmas hooks and little ones alone together.

222 ✒ Whimsical Lights

Strings of lights in the form of cows, chile peppers, bucking broncos, flamingos, and cacti, among others, are now carried by most novelty stores and lighting shops. If your tree could use a new look, some of these lights may inspire you.

HANDMADE TREE DECORATIONS

Ornaments that have been used year after year are full of memories of Christmases past. Some are heirlooms, others are gifts, but those most treasured are the handmade ones. Creating decorations for the tree is one more way to multiply the joys of Christmas.

223 ¾ Patchwork Balls

This ornament makes good use of unassembled pieces of patchwork found at flea markets or items out of your own scrap bag. Use a glue gun to cover a Styrofoam ball with bits of fabric cut out with pinking shears. For a country look use cotton; for a more formal look, velvet and taffeta. Make use of prints, polka dots, florals, and plaids, but stay in the same color family on each ball. Work slowly, overlapping the fabrics. Glue on gold or color-coordinated rickrack or ribbon or leave plain. Top with a matching bow and add a ribbon loop for hanging.

224 ¾ Patchwork Eggs

Use plastic eggs instead of balls. You can turn these into little treasure boxes for the children by filling them with tiny toy surprises. Work with the eggs open. Cover in the same way as the patchwork balls but use binding or rickrack around the egg at the opening to make it easier to find. Insert the surprise, attach a ribbon loop, and hang.

225 ¾ Mini Packs

Cover small gift boxes, the kind earrings generally come in, and cover them in scraps of wrapping paper too small for real packages. Tie each with a very thin piece of silk ribbon or gold cord and hang on the tree. You can also use these ornaments on gift-wrapped packages. Glue or wire a couple to the bow.

226 🖎 Fantastic Ornaments

Fan ornaments are very easy to construct. Cut a six- by twelve-inch piece of foil wrapping paper. (For a festive look, use printed foil paper; for a more elegant ornament, especially for a Victorian tree, use solid gold or silver foil.) Make an accordion fold every half inch. Hold the closed folded fan in the middle and cut the top and bottom to round them out. Two inches from the bottom of one end of the fan, tie a color-coordinated piece of ribbon into a bow, spread the fan and add a ribbon loop to the back for hanging. For a more elaborate fan, after rounding it out, cut a pattern, such as triangles, into the folds.

227 🖎 Victorian Doily Fans

Even easier to make are these charming gold doily fans. Cut a round doily in half. Accordion pleat the half doily into a fan and attach a cluster of small fabric or dried flowers to the front of it with glue. Attach to the tree with wire.

228   Net Balls

Turn plain into fancy with netting, lace, or other see-through fabrics. Cut a circle of fabric large enough to cover a large gold or silver Christmas ball with an extra two inches all around to gather at the top. Tie off the fabric with a bow or streamer of silver or gold ribbon to match the ornament. Using a glue gun, attach a few tiny white or gold fabric flowers or some sprigs of dried heather or lavender to the bow.

229   Nostalgic Nosegays

Nosegays are easy to make and lend a Victorian touch to your tree or your table. Use one at every setting and insert an old-fashioned place card with each name beautifully lettered in gold ink. The effect is particularly rich if you use gold doilies with burgundy, deep rose, or purple fabric flowers. Or make the nosegays with live flowers, tuck in place cards, and put one in a bud vase at each setting. Encourage guests to take the nosegays home to hang on their own tree.

Stick the stem of a fabric rose into the center of a small gold or white doily, pinch it so it gathers around the flower, then turn it over and secure tightly with tape. Tie a 12-inch length of half-inch matching ribbon once around the tape and leave the ends as streamers. Use the stem to attach to the tree. For a more romantic look, use a red heart-shape doily. You could also use a larger doily and wire together bunches of dried flowers, like tea roses, baby's breath, heather, and statice. For a seasonal touch, add some cinnamon sticks.

230   Cornucopias

The Victorians were fond of trimming the tree with cornucopias filled with dried herbs or homemade sugar plums and barley sugar candies. Make your own cornucopias and fill them with dried heather, lavender, sprigs of pine, a few shafts of wheat, or dried baby's breath.

- Cut a quarter wedge out of a white or gold doily and wrap the rest around until you have a cone shape; glue or staple together. If you wish, add a small bow and some ribbon roses to the front; attach a ribbon loop for hanging.
- For a more natural look, use handmade paper. Cut out a circle pattern twelve inches in diameter, then cut into four wedges; roll each into a cone. If you wish, stencil on some leaves or a design before forming the cone.
- Take some children's party hats in bright colors, tie the elastic into a knot to shorten it, and fill with the dried flowers or, as a treat for the children, with popcorn or small (not too heavy) Christmas candies. Hang on the tree by the elastic band; if the candy is too heavy, use a glue gun to attach a ribbon loop.

231   Buttons & Bows

Use a two-inch-wide piece of grosgrain, moire, or silk ribbon and make a batch of bows. Attach a large unusual button to the middle of the bow with a piece of thin wire threaded through the holes or shank of the button and then wrapped around the bow. Use the wire to attach the bow to the tree.

232   Handy Ornaments

Have every child in the family trace an outline of his or her hand on a piece of felt (use a different color felt for each). Cut out the hand and let the kids paint their own hand prints with glue and decorate them with glitter or foil confetti. When the hands are dry, attach a ribbon loop for hanging on the tree. Repeat the process every year, using the same color felt for each child, and watch the family grow.

233   Original Art

Clear glass Christmas balls make wonderful canvases to paint with a scene or abstract motif. Apply acrylic paint with small makeup brushes or cotton swabs. Have the artist sign or initial the work, especially if the ornament is a gift.

234   Basket Weave Paper Hearts

For an eye-catching decoration, make paper hearts out of a combination of gold foil and mat red paper or silver foil and mat blue paper. Trace the pattern on page 264 and transfer it to a three- by nine-inch piece of each of the two different papers you are using. Put one piece on top of the other and cut along the lines of the pattern. Hold the two pieces together at the rounded part and weave the strips in and out in a basket-weave design. Attach a small ribbon or paper loop to the back and hang.

235 ✿ Glittering Stars

Draw free-form stars in several sizes on wax paper with white glue (it dries hard). Sprinkle with glitter, making sure the glue is completely covered. Use red, blue, gold, and silver glitter. Allow two days for the stars to dry. Then working in from each point, carefully peel away the wax paper. Hook the stars over the branches to hang on the tree.

236 ✿ Tree Garlands

Garlands are fun for children to make. One or more of the following are a must on a traditional Christmas tree. To make the task and the hanging more manageable, work in eight- or nine-foot lengths.

- Instead of using paper to make a chain garland that you'll discard, use ribbon and store it for reuse. Cut three-inch-wide solid red or red and green plaid ribbon into eight-inch lengths, loop the ends of one piece together, and glue; loop another piece of ribbon through the finished loop and glue that. Continue until you have a long garland.
- Garlands of cranberries tend to get heavy, so work with either thin wire or heavy nylon thread.
- Use air-popped popcorn and allow it to get stale overnight for easier handling. String with cotton thread in deference to the birds who will be the beneficiaries when the tree comes down.

237 ✿ Paper Snowflakes

Fold a round white paper doily into eighths and cut designs into all three sides of the wedge. Every one you make will be different. Attach a ribbon loop to the back or just tuck into the tree branches. For more dramatic snowflakes, use silver doilies.

238 ❆ Two Easy Ornaments for Young Children to Make

• Cover the tops and bottoms of frozen juice containers with white glue and coat with glitter or fabric. Punch a hole near the edge and use a ribbon to hang on the tree.
• Use cookie cutters to outline trees, bells, reindeer, and wreaths on lightweight cardboard. Cut them out, cover them with white glue, and sprinkle green, red, or gold glitter over the glue. Punch a hole in the top and thread a piece of ribbon through or hang with a hook.

239 ❆ Paper Cutout Chains

Use paper chains of Christmas trees, snowmen, hearts, and wreaths to decorate packages or hook the chains together and loop them around the tree. Take long strips of four-inch-wide wrapping, origami, tissue, or other lightweight paper and fold each strip into accordion or fan-style folds, about two and a half inches wide. Trace one of the half patterns on pages 265 and 266, lay it on top of the folded paper, and trace the shape. Cut out carefully through all of the layers. In the case of hearts, use a paper punch to make designs the easy way before you unfold. You can also cut free-form designs.

240 ❆ Mini Yule Logs

Tie a half-inch-wide ribbon around five cinnamon sticks that you have glued together and hang from the tree.

241 ❆ Cranballs

Instead of the usual garlands of cranberries, make cranberry balls; they will stay fresh-looking for at least two weeks. Cover a small Styrofoam ball with glue, then attach fresh cranberries, slowly working in sections all the way around. Add a ribbon loop for hanging.

242 ⚡ Victorian Jewel Ornament

Take your inspiration from Queen Victoria's Fabergé eggs and create a bejeweled ornament to keep or to give as a gift.

3-inch Styrofoam ball
Gold paint
4 inches gold wire
White glue
Gold beading pins

36 inches gold braid, ¼ inch wide
Assorted gold and crystal beads
  and pearls
Gold beading
Beaded or gold tassel

1. Paint the Styrofoam ball gold and let dry overnight.
2. Form a double loop of gold wire and insert the ends into the top of the ball; glue to secure. With a glue gun and the gold pins, attach the gold braid around the ball twice to create 4 sections. Create a design with the loose beads, making each of the sections the same or completely different. Work very slowly to allow each piece to dry.

3. Attach the gold beading in loops around the bottom of the ornament. Finish off with a tassel at the very bottom of the ball.

THEME TREES

243 ❧ Natural Beauty

Leave all the glitter, color, and lights behind one year and use the muted tones of nature for your Christmas tree. Tuck into the branches bunches of dried hydrangea, heather, baby's breath, cockscomb, and yarrow. Tie clusters of lavender and cinnamon sticks with raffia and attach pinecones with florist wire. Cover the inside of tiny round baskets with sheet moss and on the outside use Spanish moss (moisten first to make it pliable) for bird's nests. If you like, add small store-bought birds. When Christmas is over, make dried floral arrangements or a wreath from the decorations.

244 ❧ Country Western Tree

This tree is a salute to the cowboy and the range. Start with strings of old-fashioned large red Christmas lights. Make a garland by knotting together red and blue bandanna neckerchiefs folded into triangles. Tie onto the branches bows of red and white gingham ribbon. Add Indian corn saved from Thanksgiving. Get a batch of sheriff's badges from a toy store and attach them to the tree with strips of rawhide. It's easy to rustle up a herd of cows, they're everywhere in the form of cow lights, cow ornaments, cow cards, and the like. Add cowboy boot cookies you've baked yourself (see page 264 for pattern).

245 ❧ Victorian Tree

The Victorians reveled in rich colors and textures. The tree that takes its inspiration from that period is sumptuously decorated with nosegays, silk tassels, paper and fabric fans, ornate blown glass ornaments, ropes of pearls and gold beads or a garland of old lace trim, gilt paper doilies, and cornucopias. The long winter evenings before the holidays were occupied with creating beautiful handmade ornaments for the trees, and the dearth of fresh flowers led to the abundant use of evergreens, especially holly, and everlastings (dried flowers) in decorating the home. Use some or all of the following for your Victorian tree:

- Dried flowers (see page 11).
- Nosegays (see page 130).
- Loose pieces from a crystal chandelier (flea market).
- Silk tassels (notions department or fabric store).
- Fans (novelty stores and flea markets; also see page 129).
- Blown glass ornaments (flea markets, antique shops, and trim-a-tree shops).
- Garlands of pearls and gold beads (craft store).
- Doilies.
- Lacy Hearts (see page 56).
- Victorian Jewel Ornament (see page 135).

246 🕭 The Christian Christmas Tree

A Christian Tree is hung with ornaments, either made or bought, each of which relates to an element of the Bible or church history. In addition to churches and angels or cherubim with wings, decorations might include some or all of the following:

- Wheat, symbol of the bread of life (Mark 14:22).
- Doves, for peace and forgiveness.
- Scrolls, representing the first five books of the Old Testament.
- An ark, symbol of the flood and of the church as refuge.
- A rainbow, sign of God's love and protection as well as His covenant with Noah and the Israelites (Genesis 9:13).
- A camel, representing the three kings.
- Musical notes, for praise and worship of the Lord.
- Grapes, for the sacrament of Holy Communion.
- A twelve-pointed star, for the twelve tribes of Israel and the twelve apostles.
- A lamb standing with the banner of victory, representing the victory of the Lord's sacrifice.

- Candles (fake or electric *never real*), to denote the Lord's words, "I am the light of the world" (John 8:12).

247 ❦ Americana Tree

Miniature American flags were typical turn-of-the-century tree decorations. Encircle the tree in white star lights and use red, white, and blue striped ribbon as a garland. Decorate with papier-mâché and wooden apple ornaments, miniature paper and cloth American flags, flag fans, and rosette bows of red, white, and blue ribbon. Add some red, blue, and silver glittering stars (see page 133). Make cloth hearts for the tree from fabrics suggesting the flag.

248 ❦ White Christmas

An all-white tree is exceedingly dramatic, but for maximum interest you need to vary the shapes and what you use to decorate it. First trim with white icicle lights, then accent the tree with ropes of silver beads, ornate silver-tone glass ornaments, two-inch-wide white sheer ribbon or crinkly paper ribbon (it comes in a coil like rope). Crumple white tissue paper and stuff it into the branches. Wire on at least two dozen dried hydrangeas. First crystallize them by spraying with fixative and sprinkling on iridescent snow confetti. For a more traditional look, spray wooden ornaments white and use store-bought Christmas doves.

249 ❦ Golden Boughs Tree

For an all-gold tree that shimmers, string with tiny yellow lights, then entwine the tree in a garland of two-inch-wide wire-edged gold ribbon. Add some golden cherubs and angels and attach gilded miniature pinecones and walnuts (see page 87). Use gold doilies to make cornucopias (see page 130) and gold foil paper to make fan ornaments (see page 129).

PART FIVE

Holiday Entertaining

CHAPTER 8

Make It Look Easy

The most basic pleasure of Christmas is the
offer of a warm welcome, of hospitality, food,
and drink. Houseguests, acquaintances, friends
and family, carolers and classmates dropping
by, all that extra company requires having a
larder that is more full than usual. The
standbys and prepare-ahead dishes
suggested in this chapter enable you to have
enough on hand for any and all guests and
to make even the most reluctant of chefs
look good.

250 🍎 Baked Apple Pancake with Caramel Sauce

PREP: 10 minutes   COOK: 20 minutes   SERVES: 6 to 8

6 eggs
⅓ cup packed brown sugar
1 stick (4 ounces) unsalted butter,
    melted
1¼ cups half-and-half
2 tablespoons Grand Marnier or
    other orange liqueur
1 cup flour

1 teaspoon vanilla extract
1 teaspoon cinnamon
¼ teaspoon salt
3 medium Granny Smith apples,
    peeled, cored, and thinly sliced
1¼ cups granulated sugar
½ cup heavy cream

1. Preheat oven to 375°F. In a large bowl, combine eggs and brown sugar. Whisk until well blended. Beat in 3 tablespoons melted butter, half-and-half, Grand Marnier, flour, vanilla, cinnamon, and salt.

2. In a 9- x 13-inch baking pan, toss remaining 5 tablespoons butter with apple slices. Sprinkle with ¼ cup granulated sugar. Bake 2 minutes.

3. Open oven and pour batter over apples. Bake 20 minutes, or until golden and slightly puffy.

4. Meanwhile, in a heavy medium saucepan, combine remaining 1 cup granulated sugar and ¼ cup water. Cook over medium heat, stirring to dissolve sugar before mixture boils. Boil syrup until golden in color, about 5 minutes. Immediately remove pan from heat and whisk in cream.

5. Serve apple pancake immediately while puffed and hot. Pass caramel sauce on the side.

251 ⚡ Overnight French Toast

PREP: 5 minutes   COOK: 15 minutes   SERVES: 6

8 slices egg or raisin bread
6 eggs
⅓ cup sugar
2 cups eggnog or buttermilk
1 teaspoon grated nutmeg

½ teaspoon cinnamon
2 tablespoons unsalted butter,
  melted and cooled
Maple syrup, as accompaniment

1. Arrange bread in a single layer in a 13- X 9- X 2-inch baking pan.

2. In a medium bowl, whisk eggs until blended. Whisk in sugar, eggnog, nutmeg, cinnamon, and butter. Pour mixture over bread. Turn slices to coat. Cover with plastic wrap and refrigerate overnight.

3. Preheat oven to 400°F. Bake 10 minutes. Turn bread over and bake until golden in color, 5 minutes. Serve with maple syrup.

252 🔥 Cheesebread Soufflé

PREP: 10 minutes   BAKE: 30 minutes   SERVES: 6 to 8

More of a savory bread pudding than a soufflé, this golden puffed casserole makes a fabulous brunch dish. It can be completely assembled ahead of time and baked at the last minute.

3 tablespoons butter
1 medium onion, finely chopped
2 cups shredded Cheddar cheese
    (about 8 ounces)
½ teaspoon dry mustard

½ teaspoon salt
¼ teaspoon pepper
10 slices firm-textured white
    bread
2 cups milk

1. Preheat oven to 350°F. In a medium saucepan, melt butter over medium heat. Add onion and cook until softened and translucent, about 3 minutes. Add cheese, mustard, salt, and pepper. Remove from heat and stir until smooth and well blended.

2. Arrange half of bread in a buttered 9- X 13-inch baking dish, tearing slices to fit if necessary to just cover bottom. Spread half of cheese mixture over bread. Cover with remaining bread and top with remaining cheese mixture. Pour milk over all.

3. Bake 30 minutes, or until brown and puffy. Serve at once.

253 🔥 Mexican Corn Frittata

PREP: 5 minutes   BAKE: 25 to 30 minutes
SERVES: 6 to 8

Everyone enjoys this brunch dish. Serve it with salsa, sour cream, and guacamole.

1 stick (4 ounces) butter
12 eggs
1 (16-ounce) can creamed corn
1 (7-ounce) can chopped green
    chiles
1 pound Cheddar cheese, shred-
    ded (about 4 cups)

1 garlic clove, crushed through a
    press
Dash Worcestershire sauce
¼ teaspoon pepper

1. Preheat oven to 375°F. Melt butter in a 9- x 13-inch baking dish in oven.

2. In a large bowl, beat eggs until blended. Stir in corn, chiles,
cheese, garlic, Worcestershire, and pepper. Pour mixture into
baking dish.

3. Bake 25 to 30 minutes, or until puffed and firm. Cut into
squares and serve at once.

254 🕮 Cottage Cheese and Chive Quiche

PREP: 5 minutes   BAKE: 42 to 44 minutes   SERVES: 8

This is lighter than traditional quiche but just as easy to make,
and it can be frozen. Reheat, covered, in the oven after it has
completely thawed.

1 (9-inch) unbaked pastry crust
2 cups cottage cheese
1 cup shredded Cheddar cheese
    (about 4 ounces)

2 eggs, lightly beaten
1 tablespoon chopped chives
¼ teaspoon salt
¼ teaspoon pepper

1. Preheat oven to 400°F. Bake pastry shell 12 to 14 minutes,
or until golden. Remove from oven and reduce oven temperature to 350°.

2. In a medium bowl, combine cottage cheese, Cheddar
cheese, eggs, chives, salt, and pepper. Mix until well blended.
Spread filling into pastry shell.

3. Bake 30 minutes, or until firm and golden. Serve hot.

255 ⟨✲ Orange Raised Waffles

PREP: 10 minutes   RISE: Overnight
BAKE: 2 to 3 minutes each   MAKES: 8

The basic batter will keep in the refrigerator for several days. Add the eggs, baking powder, vanilla, and orange zest just before making the waffles.

*1 envelope (¼ ounce) active dry
    yeast*
*½ cup warm water (105°to
    115°F)*
*2 cups warm milk (105°to
    115°F)*
1 stick (4 ounces) butter, melted
½ teaspoon salt

1 teaspoon sugar
2 cups flour
2 eggs, lightly beaten
¼ teaspoon baking powder
1 teaspoon vanilla extract
1 tablespoon grated orange zest
*Maple syrup and butter, as
    accompaniment*

1. In a large bowl, dissolve yeast in warm water. Stir in milk, melted butter, salt, sugar, and flour until smooth. Cover with plastic wrap and let stand overnight at room temperature.

2. Preheat waffle iron according to manufacturer's instructions. Add eggs, baking powder, vanilla, and orange zest to batter and blend well.

3. Ladle batter into waffle iron. Bake 2 to 3 minutes, or until golden brown. Repeat with remaining batter. Serve hot with maple syrup and butter.

256 ✿ Mushrooms Stuffed with Crab

PREP: 20 minutes   COOK: 13 minutes   MAKES: 24

This timeless combination is always a favorite with guests.

24 medium mushrooms (about
   1 pound)
3 tablespoons butter or olive oil
1 shallot, minced
1 (8-ounce) package cream cheese,
   softened
1 (6-ounce) can crabmeat

1 tablespoon lemon juice
1 tablespoon minced parsley
½ teaspoon prepared white horseradish
¼ teaspoon salt
Dash of cayenne

1. Preheat oven to 375°F. Remove stems from mushrooms and finely chop. In a medium skillet, melt 1 tablespoon butter over medium heat. Add shallot and mushroom stems and cook until mushroom liquid is exuded and then evaporates, about 3 minutes. Scrape mixture into a medium bowl. Add cream cheese, crabmeat, lemon juice, parsley, horseradish, salt, and cayenne. Blend well.

2. In same skillet, melt remaining 2 tablespoons butter over medium heat. Immediately remove from heat and toss mushroom caps in butter until well coated. Arrange caps stem ends up on a baking sheet and mound about 2 teaspoons crab filling in each. (If made in advance, cover with plastic wrap and refrigerate up to 8 hours.)

3. Bake 10 minutes, or until filling is bubbly and mushrooms are tender but still hold their shape.

257 ❦ Fruited Cheese Spread

PREP: 10 minutes   COOK: 10 to 12 minutes   MAKES: 1½ cups

This spread is good on crackers or on moist date or banana bread.

½ cup coarsely chopped walnuts
1 (8-ounce) package cream cheese,
    softened

¾ cup dried cranberries or raisins

1. Preheat oven to 325°F. Spread walnuts on a baking sheet and bake until fragrant and lightly browned, 10 to 12 minutes. Let cool.
2. In a small bowl, combine toasted walnuts with cream cheese and dried cranberries. Mix until well blended. If made in advance, cover and refrigerate up to 3 days.

258 ❦ Black Bean Soup

PREP: 15 minutes   STAND: overnight   COOK: 4 hours
SERVES: 8

A big pot of savory black bean soup simmering on the stove is great for holiday drop-ins. Ladled into cups rather than mugs, it will serve up to 16 people. Dress up the soup by offering garnishes of dry sherry, chopped egg, and onion, or sour cream and salsa.

1 pound dried black beans, rinsed
    and picked over
1 ham bone or smoked ham hock
1 bay leaf
1 large onion, chopped
3 garlic cloves, finely chopped
¼ cup olive oil, preferably extra
    virgin

1 medium green bell pepper, diced
1 red bell pepper, diced
½ cup tomato sauce
¾ teaspoon dried oregano
¾ teaspoon ground cumin
1½ teaspoons salt
½ teaspoon freshly ground pepper
2 tablespoons cider vinegar

1. In a large pot, soak beans in water to cover by at least 2 inches overnight; drain. Return beans to pot and add 3 quarts water, ham bone, and bay leaf. Bring to a boil, reduce heat to medium-low, and simmer, covered, 3 hours.

2. Meanwhile, in a large skillet, cook onion and garlic in olive oil over medium heat, stirring occasionally, until softened and translucent, about 3 minutes. Add green and red peppers and cook until softened, 2 to 3 minutes.

3. Scrape sautéed vegetables with olive oil into soup. Add tomato sauce, oregano, cumin, salt, pepper, and vinegar. If soup is too thick, add additional water. Simmer 1 hour longer. Remove and discard bay leaf and ham bone. Season soup with additional salt and pepper to taste.

259 ✦ Scalloped Oysters

PREP: 5 minutes   BAKE: 20 to 25 minutes   SERVES: 6 to 8

Here's a traditional New England dish that can complement any turkey dinner.

2 cups oyster crackers
1 pint oysters
½ cup heavy cream
¼ teaspoon salt

⅛ teaspoon freshly ground pepper
1 tablespoon chopped parsley
2 tablespoons butter

1. Preheat oven to 425°F. Butter a 9- X 13-inch glass baking dish.

2. Layer bottom of dish with half of crackers. Top with oysters. Drizzle ¼ cup cream over oysters and season with half of salt and pepper. Sprinkle on parsley. Top with remaining crackers, cream, and salt and pepper. Dot with butter.

3. Bake 20 to 25 minutes, or until bubbly and lightly browned.

260 🌿 Carrot Puree with Bourbon

PREP: 20 minutes   COOK: 7 to 9 minutes   SERVES: 8 to 10

This colorful side dish is kind to the cook, since it can be made up to two days in advance and reheated.

3 pounds carrots, peeled and cut into 1-inch pieces
1 stick (4 ounces) butter, cut into 8 pieces and softened
1½ teaspoons salt
½ teaspoon white pepper
½ teaspoon sugar
¼ teaspoon grated nutmeg
¼ cup heavy cream
2 tablespoons bourbon

1. In a large saucepan of boiling salted water, cook carrots until tender, 7 to 9 minutes. Drain.

2. In a food processor, finely chop one-third of carrots. Add remaining carrots in 2 batches, processing until a coarse paste forms. Add butter, salt, pepper, sugar, and nutmeg and process until well blended. Add cream and bourbon and process until smooth.

3. Serve immediately, or cover and refrigerate up to 2 days. Reheat in a microwave or double boiler.

261 🌿 Polenta with Cranberries and Tangerines

PREP: 10 minutes   COOK: 5 to 10 minutes   SERVES: 8

This unusual combination was inspired by Molly Chappellet, a renowned California artist and cook. Serve with turkey and no one will miss the traditional mashed potatoes and cranberry sauce.

2 medium tangerines, cut into 1-inch pieces (skins left on) and seeded
1 (12-ounce) bag cranberries
½ cup sugar
½ teaspoon salt
¾ cup instant polenta or yellow cornmeal

1. In a food processor, coarsely chop tangerines. Add cranberries and sugar and pulse until finely chopped but not mushy.

2. In a medium saucepan, combine 4 cups water and salt over high heat. When water boils, whisk in polenta in a slow, steady stream. Reduce heat to medium and cook, stirring, until polenta is thickened to consistency of hot cereal, 5 to 10 minutes. Stir in cranberry-tangerine mixture and serve immediately.

262   Mashed Potato Casserole with Pesto

PREP: 20 minutes   COOK: 55 to 60 minutes   SERVES: 8

8 to 10 medium baking potatoes (about 3½ pounds)
1 (8-ounce) package cream cheese, softened
¼ cup sour cream
Salt and freshly ground pepper
Pesto (recipe follows)
2 tablespoons melted butter or olive oil

1. In a large pot of boiling salted water, cook potatoes until tender, 25 to 30 minutes. Drain, then peel when cool enough to handle.

2. In a large bowl, with an electric mixer on medium speed, beat cream cheese with sour cream until blended. Gradually add drained hot potatoes, beating until smooth and soft. Season with salt and pepper to taste.

3. Spoon about one-fourth of whipped potatoes into a buttered 2-quart ovenproof casserole and top with one-third of pesto. Repeat layers of potatoes and pesto, ending with potatoes. Brush surface with melted butter or olive oil. (Recipe can be made a day ahead. If made only a few hours before serving, refrigeration is unnecessary; leave in a cool spot at room temperature. If refrigerated, return to room temperature before baking.)

4. Preheat oven to 350°F. Bake mashed potatoes until heated through, about 30 minutes.

263 🌢 Pesto

PREP: 5 minutes   COOK: none   MAKES: about 1 cup

*1 cup lightly packed fresh basil
  leaves
1 large garlic clove, minced
¼ cup grated Parmesan cheese*

*⅓ cup extra-virgin olive oil
1 tablespoon pine nuts (pignoli)
¼ teaspoon salt
⅛ teaspoon freshly ground pepper*

In a food processor or blender, combine basil, garlic, Parmesan cheese, olive oil, pine nuts, salt, and pepper. Puree until smooth. If made in advance, cover and refrigerate up to 4 days or freeze.

264 🌢 Sweet Potato Puff

PREP: 45 minutes   BAKE: 30 minutes   SERVES: 8

*4 large sweet potatoes
½ cup half-and-half
⅓ cup honey
¼ cup brandy
4 tablespoons butter, softened*

*1 teaspoon grated orange zest
½ teaspoon cinnamon
¼ teaspoon grated nutmeg
4 eggs, separated*

1. In a pot of boiling water, cook sweet potatoes until tender, 35 to 40 minutes; drain. As soon as they are cool enough to handle, peel.

2. Preheat oven to 400°F. Butter a 6-cup soufflé dish. Heat half-and-half to a simmer.

3. In a large bowl, mash sweet potatoes. Mix in half-and-half, honey, brandy, and butter until thoroughly combined. Add orange zest, cinnamon, nutmeg, and yolks; blend well.

4. In a large bowl, using a hand-held electric mixer, beat egg whites on medium speed until soft peaks form. Increase speed to high and continue beating until stiff peaks form. Fold into sweet potatoes. Turn into prepared soufflé dish and bake 30 minutes, until puffed. Serve immediately.

265 🔪 Baked Risotto

PREP: 10 minutes   COOK: 23 to 24 minutes   SERVES: 6

This alternative to the traditional stovetop method allows the cook a free hand in the kitchen.

4 tablespoons butter
1 small onion, chopped
1½ cups Arborio rice
3 cups chicken broth

¼ cup grated Parmesan cheese
⅛ teaspoon freshly ground pepper
Salt

1. Preheat oven to 425°F. In a medium ovenproof saucepan or flameproof casserole, melt butter over medium heat. Add onion and cook until softened but not browned, 2 to 3 minutes. Add rice and cook, stirring, for 1 minute. Stir in broth and bring to a boil.

2. Place saucepan in oven and bake, covered, until rice is creamy and tender but still firm in center, about 20 minutes. Stir in cheese and pepper. Add salt to taste. Serve immediately.

266 🌰 Almond Christmas Wreath Bread

PREP: 15 minutes   STAND: 2¼ hours   BAKE: 20 to 25 minutes
MAKES: 1 loaf

Yeast doughs do take time to rise, but this slightly sweet loaf is so pretty and so good for breakfast or with coffee, it's worth the wait.

1 envelope (¼ ounce) active dry
    yeast
¼ cup warm water (105°to
    115°F)
½ cup warm milk
3 tablespoons honey
4 tablespoons butter, softened
1 teaspoon salt

½ teaspoon ground cardamom
2 eggs
1½ teaspoons grated lemon zest
3½ cups flour
Almond Filling (recipe follows)
⅔ cup powdered sugar
1½ teaspoons lemon juice

1. In a large bowl, dissolve yeast in warm water. Add milk, honey, butter, salt, cardamom, eggs, and lemon zest. Beat until well blended. Gradually mix in 3¼ cups of flour. Turn out onto a floured work surface and knead until smooth and elastic, 10 to 15 minutes, adding remaining flour as necessary if dough sticks. Place in a clean large bowl, cover with a damp kitchen towel, and let rise until doubled, about 1½ hours.

2. Grease and flour a cookie sheet. Punch down dough. On a lightly floured surface, roll out dough into a 9- X 30-inch rectangle. Sprinkle filling to within 1 inch of edges. Starting from a long side, tightly roll up dough. Moisten edge with water and pinch to seal.

3. Using a floured knife, cut roll lengthwise in half. With cut sides up, twist ropes around each other to form a single piece. Slide onto cookie sheet and shape dough into a circle. Pinch ends to seal.

4. Let rise, uncovered, until dough is light and almost doubled, about 45 minutes. Fifteen minutes before end of rising time, preheat oven to 375°F.

5. Bake bread 20 to 30 minutes, or until lightly browned. Let cool on a rack.

6. In a small bowl, combine powdered sugar, lemon juice, and 1 tablespoon water. Stir together until smooth and well blended. Drizzle glaze over cooled bread.

Almond Filling

PREP: 5 minutes   COOK: none   MAKES: about 1½ cups

4 tablespoons butter, softened
¼ cup flour
2 tablespoons granulated sugar
⅔ cup chopped blanched almonds

½ teaspoon grated lemon zest
¾ teaspoon almond extract
½ cup glacé cherries, chopped

In a medium bowl, mix together butter, flour, and sugar until very well blended. Stir in almonds, lemon zest, almond extract, and cherries. Cover and refrigerate until ready to use.

267 🖋 Anadama Date and Walnut Bread

PREP: 10 minutes   RISE: 2 hours 15 minutes
BAKE: 35 to 40 minutes   MAKES: 1 round loaf

1 envelope (¼ ounce) active dry
    yeast
1 cup plus 1 tablespoon warm
    water (105°to 115°F)
⅓ cup light molasses
2½ tablespoons vegetable oil
1½ cups whole wheat flour

¾ cup yellow cornmeal
¾ teaspoon salt
½ teaspoon baking soda
2½ cups all-purpose flour
1 cup pitted dates
½ cup coarsely chopped walnuts

1. In a large bowl, dissolve yeast in water. Add molasses and oil. Stir in whole wheat flour, cornmeal, salt, baking soda, and all-purpose flour until a stiff dough forms. Turn out onto a floured work surface and knead 10 to 15 minutes, or until a smooth, elastic dough forms. Knead in dates and walnuts. Place in a bowl, cover with a kitchen towel, and let rise 1½ hours, or until doubled.

2. Grease a 9-inch pie pan and sprinkle lightly with additional cornmeal. Punch down dough and form into a ball. Place, smooth side up, in pie pan, cover with a towel and let rise until doubled, about 45 minutes. Preheat oven to 350°F.

3. Bake 35 to 40 minutes, or until golden brown. Let cool on a rack. Serve warm with butter.

268 ✒ Brown Bread with Raisins

PREP: 10 minutes   BAKE: 1 hour 20 minutes   SERVES: 8 to 10

This nutritious bread is wonderful with sausage, beans, and beer. It is also very good spread with cream cheese.

3 tablespoons butter, softened
¾ cup packed brown sugar
2 cups buttermilk
3 tablespoons light molasses
2 cups whole wheat flour

½ cup wheat germ
2 teaspoons baking soda
1 teaspoon salt
¾ cup raisins

1. Preheat oven to 350°F. Grease and flour a 9- x 5- x 3-inch loaf pan.

2. In a large bowl, beat butter and brown sugar until smooth. Blend in buttermilk and molasses. In a separate bowl, stir together flour, wheat germ, baking soda, and salt. Add raisins and toss to mix. Add dry ingredients to liquid ingredients and stir until well combined. Spoon into pan.

3. Bake 1 hour 20 minutes, or until a toothpick inserted in center comes out clean. Let cool 30 minutes in pan, then unmold and finish cooling on a rack.

269 ⚘ Cinnamon, Raisin, and Walnut Batter Bread

PREP: 10 minutes   RISE: 40 to 50 minutes
BAKE: 30 to 35 minutes   SERVES: 10 to 12

This yeast bread doesn't require kneading, and it rises quickly. This bread is wonderful still warm from the oven, but the next day it is just as delicious toasted and spread with sweet butter.

*1 envelope (¼ ounce) active dry
    yeast
1½ cups warm water (105°to
    115°F)
2 tablespoons honey
2 cups whole wheat flour*

*1 cup all-purpose flour
1 teaspoon cinnamon
1 teaspoon salt
2 tablespoons butter, softened
1 cup raisins
½ cup chopped toasted walnuts*

1. In a large bowl, dissolve yeast in water. Whisk in honey.
2. Stir in whole wheat flour, all-purpose flour, cinnamon, and salt until well blended. Add butter, raisins, and walnuts and mix well.
3. Cover bowl with a kitchen towel and let dough rise in a warm, draft-free place 40 to 50 minutes, or until doubled.
4. Stir dough down with a spoon and place in a generously greased 9- x 5- x 3-inch loaf pan. Cover and let rise in a warm place 20 to 30 minutes, or until dough has reached top of pan. About 15 minutes before end of rising time, preheat oven to 400°F.
5. Bake 30 to 35 minutes, or until top of bread is golden and bottom sounds hollow when tapped. Immediately remove from pan and let cool on a rack.

270 🌾 Potato Rosemary Bread

PREP: 15 minutes   RISE: 1½ hours   BAKE: 45 to 50 minutes
MAKES: 1 round loaf

*2 medium baking potatoes, peeled
    and cut into 1-inch chunks
½ teaspoon minced rosemary
1 envelope (¼ ounce) active dry
    yeast*

*½ teaspoon salt
½ teaspoon pepper
2 cups flour*

1. In a medium saucepan, cook potatoes in boiling water until tender, about 15 minutes. Drain, reserving 1¼ cups of cooking water. Pour cooking water into a large bowl, add rosemary, and let cool until tepid. Add yeast and let stand 5 to 10 minutes to dissolve.

2. Add salt, pepper, and flour to yeast mixture, stirring to make a firm dough. Turn out onto a lightly floured work surface and knead 15 to 20 minutes, or until dough is smooth and pliable. Work mashed potatoes into dough.

3. Put dough in a clean large bowl, cover with a kitchen towel and let rise 1 hour, or until doubled in size. Punch down, shape into a round loaf, and place on a greased baking sheet. Let rise 30 minutes, or until doubled in size. About 15 minutes before end of rising time, preheat oven to 350°F.

4. Bake loaf 15 minutes. For extra-crisp crust, spray loaf and oven generously with water (a clean plant sprayer does job well). Bake 30 to 35 minutes longer, or until top of loaf is brown and bottom sounds hollow when tapped.

271 🐿 Pumpkin Muffins

PREP: 10 minutes   BAKE: 20 to 25 minutes   MAKES: 18

1 cup packed brown sugar
¾ cup vegetable oil
3 eggs
1½ cups canned pumpkin puree
3½ cups flour
2 teaspoons baking powder
1 teaspoon baking soda

1 teaspoon cinnamon
1 teaspoon grated nutmeg
½ teaspoon ground cloves
¼ teaspoon salt
1 cup unsweetened apple juice
½ cup chopped toasted walnuts
½ cup raisins

1. Preheat oven to 375°F. Grease 18 muffin cups or line with paper baking cups.

2. In a large bowl, using a hand-held electric mixer, beat brown sugar and oil until light and fluffy. Add eggs, one at a time, beating well after each addition. Add pumpkin puree and mix until combined.

3. In a medium bowl, combine flour, baking powder, baking soda, cinnamon, nutmeg, cloves, and salt. Stir or whisk gently to mix. Alternately add dry ingredients and juice to pumpkin mixture, beginning and ending with dry ingredients. Stir in walnuts and raisins.

4. Pour batter into muffin cups. Bake until tops are golden and springy to touch, 20 to 25 minutes.

272 🐦 Yogurt and Blueberry Scones

PREP: 10 minutes   BAKE: 12 to 15 minutes   MAKES: 10

Serve these flaky scones hot from the oven with sweet butter and your favorite jam. They are equally good for breakfast, teatime, or a late-night snack.

3 cups flour
2 teaspoons baking powder
1 teaspoon baking soda
½ teaspoon salt
2 tablespoons brown sugar

6 tablespoons cold butter
1¼ cups plain yogurt
2 eggs
½ cup blueberries, fresh or frozen
¼ teaspoon cinnamon

1. Preheat oven to 400°F. Grease a cookie sheet. In a medium bowl, combine flour, baking powder, baking soda, salt, and brown sugar. Stir or whisk gently until well mixed. Grate cold butter into flour mixture by using largest holes on a box grater, stirring butter in as you grate so it will not stick together.

2. Make a well in center and add yogurt and 1 egg. Dust blueberries with cinnamon and add to dough. Stir until just combined. Use a ¼-cup measure to scoop dough onto cookie sheet. Beat remaining egg and brush on top of each scone.

3. Bake 12 to 15 minutes, or until golden brown. Serve immediately.

CHAPTER 9

The Many Feasts of Christmas

Good friends, good cheer, good conversation
are the true gifts of yuletide, that's why
holiday entertaining is so important to both
host and guest. No matter what your style of
entertaining, you'll find menus in this chapter
that are sure crowd pleasers. In addition to a
Holiday Cocktail Party and a Christmas Eve
Open House, there are menus for a Children's
Christmas Table, a Victorian Christmas
Dinner with roast goose as its centerpiece, a
Traditional Christmas Dinner featuring turkey
with a savory stuffing, and an Irish Hunt
Breakfast. You'll also find two excuses to
extend the holiday festivities with a Boxing
Day Supper, observed in England on
December 26, and a Twelfth Night Dessert
Party, to be held on January 6.

HOLIDAY COCKTAIL PARTY

SERVES: AT LEAST 24

Choose as many of the following recipes as you feel you'd like to make, depending upon your time and the number of guests you want to invite. Fill in with purchased items, and be sure to allow yourself a little time to relax before the party.

Wassail

Sweet and Salted Almonds
Spiced Green Olives
Crudités with Assorted Dips
Creamy Crab Dip
Piquant Curry Dip
Water Chestnut Dip
Zesty Smoked Salmon Spread
Cucumbers Stuffed with Feta Cheese
Mushroom and Ricotta Tartlets
Bell Pepper Mini Quiches
Artichoke Quiche
Brioche Basket Filled with Brie

273 🎄 Wassail

PREP: 5 minutes   COOK: 20 minutes
MAKES: about 25 (4–ounce) servings

You can make two different versions of this ancient holiday beverage from this recipe. Whisking in a little milk will give your wassail the traditional "lamb's wool" look. This type of wassail is traditionally garnished with little baked apples. If you leave out the milk, garnish the bowl with clove-studded orange slices. Reduce the chances of cracking a crystal punch bowl by filling the bowl with warm water and letting it stand for several minutes. Drain at the last second and slowly pour in the hot wassail.

6 lady apples or other very small apples or 2 oranges and about 24 cloves
1 (3-inch) cinnamon stick
3 whole allspice berries
3 whole cardamom pods
3 whole cloves

⅛ whole nutmeg or ¼ teaspoon grated
2 liters ginger ale
1 (750-ml) bottle cream sherry
1 cup brandy
1 cup milk (optional)

1. Preheat oven to 350°F. Rinse apples, put them on a cookie sheet, and bake until brown and tender, 20 minutes or longer, depending on size. Or slice oranges and stud peel with cloves.

2. Break up cinnamon stick and lightly crush allspice berries and cardamom pods with back of a spoon. Wrap cinnamon, allspice, cardamom, cloves, and nutmeg in several thicknesses of cheesecloth and tie securely with white cotton string.

3. Put spice bag in a large nonreactive saucepan with 2 cups ginger ale. Heat to boiling, reduce heat, and simmer 10 minutes. Remove and discard spice bag. Add remaining ginger ale, sherry, and brandy to pot and heat until mixture is steaming hot, but do not boil. Whisk in milk, if desired, and pour into a punch bowl.

4. Garnish bowl with either baked apples or clove-studded orange slices. Serve at once.

274 ⚜ Sweet and Salted Almonds

PREP: 10 minutes   COOK: 10 to 15 minutes   MAKES: 2 cups

This nibble also makes a wonderful hostess gift for the holidays. For a large party, make a double batch and set out several bowls around the room.

2 cups whole blanched almonds   ½ teaspoon salt
1 tablespoon extra-virgin olive oil   ½ teaspoon sugar

1. Preheat oven to 350°F. Spread almonds on a baking sheet. Drizzle with oil and toss to coat. Roast for 10 to 15 minutes, tossing occasionally, until light golden brown.

2. On the baking sheet, toss warm almonds with salt and sugar. Let cool. Drain almonds on paper towels to remove excess oil. If made in advance, store airtight up to 2 weeks.

275 ⚜ Spiced Green Olives

PREP: 10 minutes   COOK: about 5 minutes   MAKES: 2 cups

Serve a few well-seasoned olives as a light appetizer before an elaborate dinner or with cocktails.

6 tablespoons extra-virgin olive oil   2 tablespoons sherry vinegar or
2 garlic cloves, crushed through a   white wine vinegar
   press   ½ teaspoon ground cumin
1 (16-ounce) jar pimiento-stuffed   ¼ teaspoon crushed hot red pepper
   green olives, drained   2 tablespoons minced parsley.

1. In a medium nonreactive saucepan, combine olive oil and garlic. Cook over low heat until garlic is fragrant, 2 to 3 minutes.

2. Stir in olives, vinegar, cumin, and hot pepper and cook until warmed through, 2 to 3 minutes.

3. Let cool, then stir in parsley. If made in advance, cover and refrigerate up to 3 days. Serve at room temperature.

276 🐚 Creamy Crab Dip

PREP: 5 minutes   COOK: 15 minutes   MAKES: 2 cups

Keep these ingredients on hand and you'll always have the makings for a quick dip for crackers or vegetables.

1 (8-ounce) package cream cheese,
  softened
1 (6-ounce) can crabmeat
2 tablespoons grated onion
1 tablespoon milk
½ teaspoon prepared white horse-

radish
½ teaspoon salt
¼ teaspoon pepper
¼ teaspoon Worcestershire sauce
Paprika

1. Preheat oven to 375°F. In a medium bowl, combine cream cheese, crabmeat, onion, milk, horseradish, salt, pepper, and Worcestershire sauce. Stir until well blended.
2. Place mixture in an ovenproof serving dish and sprinkle with paprika. Bake until heated through, about 15 minutes.

277 🐚 Piquant Curry Dip

PREP: 5 minutes   COOK: none   MAKES: 1½ cups

Serve this spicy dipping sauce with carrot sticks and cauliflower florets. The bitters lend an intriguing taste.

¾ cup mayonnaise
¾ cup sour cream
2 scallions, minced
1 tablespoon lime or lemon juice
2 teaspoons curry powder
1 teaspoon paprika

1 teaspoon Worcestershire sauce
1 teaspoon aromatic bitters, such
  as Angostura
1 teaspoon Dijon mustard
⅛ teaspoon hot pepper sauce

In a small bowl, combine all the ingredients and stir until well blended. If made in advance, cover and refrigerate up to 3 days.

278 🥄 Water Chestnut Dip

PREP: 5 minutes   COOK: none   CHILL: 2 hours
MAKES: 2½ cups

This crunchy dip with Asian overtones is perfect with an assortment of crisp raw vegetables, such as broccoli and snow peas.

1 cup mayonnaise
1 cup sour cream
1 (8-ounce) can water chestnuts, drained and coarsely chopped
¼ cup minced cilantro or parsley
¼ cup chopped scallions
1 tablespoon soy sauce
Dash hot pepper sauce
½ teaspoon toasted sesame seeds

1. In a medium bowl, combine mayonnaise, sour cream, water chestnuts, cilantro, scallions, soy sauce, and hot sauce. Stir until well blended.
2. Cover and refrigerate 2 hours or as long as overnight. Before serving, sprinkle sesame seeds on top.

279 🥄 Zesty Smoked Salmon Spread

PREP: 5 minutes   COOK: none   MAKES: about 2½ cups

Serve this flavorful spread with fresh miniature bagel halves, bagel chips, cocktail rye bread, or cucumber slices.

2 (8-ounce) packages cream cheese, softened
6 ounces smoked salmon
3 scallions, coarsely chopped
1 tablespoon lemon juice
1 teaspoon prepared white horseradish
¼ teaspoon salt
¼ teaspoon freshly ground black pepper

In a food processor, combine all ingredients and process until well mixed. If made in advance, cover and refrigerate up to 3 days. Serve at room temperature.

280 ₦ Cucumbers Stuffed with Feta Cheese

PREP: 10 minutes   COOK: none   CHILL: 24 hours   MAKES: 48

The assertive flavor of feta cheese goes well with cool, crisp cucumbers.

2 medium English (hothouse)
  cucumbers, scrubbed
1 (8-ounce) package cream cheese,
  softened

½ cup crumbled feta cheese
2 tablespoons chopped fresh dill or
  2 teaspoons dried

1. Remove ends from cucumbers and cut in half lengthwise. Using a melon baller or grapefruit spoon, remove seeds from both halves. Set aside. In a small bowl, combine cream cheese, feta cheese, and dill. Blend until well mixed.

2. Stuff each cucumber half with cheese mixture and reassemble halves, pressing together gently. Wrap in plastic wrap and refrigerate overnight.

3. Before serving, cut cucumbers into ½-inch slices.

281 ⚜ Mushroom and Ricotta Tartlets

PREP: 30 minutes   BAKE: 20 minutes   MAKES: 24

1½ sticks (6 ounces) butter, melted
1 pound mushrooms, sliced
4 eggs, beaten
1 pound ricotta cheese
½ cup heavy cream

½ teaspoon dried thyme
1 teaspoon salt
½ teaspoon pepper
8 sheets of filo dough, thawed according to package directions

1. Preheat oven to 375°F. Grease 24 muffin cups.

2. In a large skillet, melt 5 tablespoons butter over medium-high heat. Add mushrooms and cook until tender, about 5 minutes. Remove with a slotted spoon and let cool.

3. In a large bowl, combine eggs, ricotta cheese, cream, thyme, salt, and pepper. Mix until smooth. Stir in sautéed mushrooms.

4. Place a sheet of filo on a work surface. Cover remaining sheets with a slightly damp towel or a piece of plastic wrap. Brush filo sheet lightly with some melted butter. Top with another sheet of filo and brush with butter. Repeat procedure with remaining 2 sheets of filo. Cut stacked filo sheets into 12 rectangles, cutting 3 strips in one direction and 4 in the other.

5. Fit each filo stack into a muffin cup, pressing against bottom and sides. Spoon mushroom filling evenly into cups. Trim edges, if ragged, with kitchen scissors.

6. Bake 20 minutes, until golden brown. Serve hot, warm, or at room temperature.

282 ❦ Bell Pepper Mini Quiches

PREP: 25 minutes   BAKE: 15 minutes   MAKES: 48

A combination of red and green bell peppers makes a colorful appetizer for holiday time.

Vegetable cooking spray
Cream Cheese Pastry (recipe follows)
1 tablespoon butter or olive oil
1 cup chopped red and green bell
   pepper
1 large garlic clove, crushed
   through a press
1 teaspoon chopped fresh thyme or
   ¼ teaspoon dried

1 cup chopped or shredded fontina
   or Swiss cheese (about
   4 ounces)
4 eggs
1 cup heavy cream
⅛ teaspoon salt
Dash of cayenne
Dash of grated nutmeg

1. Preheat oven to 400°F. Oil insides of 48 mini muffin cups with vegetable cooking spray. Press 2 teaspoons pastry evenly into each muffin cup to line bottom and sides. Refrigerate.

2. In a medium skillet, heat butter over medium heat. Add pepper and garlic and cook until softened but not browned, about 3 minutes. Remove from heat, stir in thyme, and let cool.

3. Distribute bell pepper mixture and cheese evenly among pastry shells. In a medium bowl, beat together eggs, cream, salt, cayenne, and nutmeg. Ladle into pastry shells.

4. Bake 15 minutes, or until filling is puffed and golden and pastry is lightly browned. Serve warm or at room temperature. (Baked mini quiches can be refrigerated up to 3 days or frozen. Reheat in a 400° oven for 5 to 10 minutes before serving.)

283 ❦ Cream Cheese Pastry

PREP: 5 minutes   COOK: none   CHILL: 2 hours
MAKES: ½ pound

1 stick (4 ounces) butter, softened
1 (3-ounce) package cream cheese,
  softened

1 cup flour
⅛ teaspoon salt
Dash cayenne

In a medium bowl or in a food processor, blend butter and cream cheese. Mix in flour, salt, and cayenne until well blended. Form into a ball, wrap in plastic wrap, and refrigerate 2 hours or overnight. Freeze for longer storage.

284 🥬 Artichoke Quiche

PREP: 20 minutes   BAKE: 35 minutes   SERVES: 6 to 8

For a large pastry, make two or three of these tasty pies. To save time, use thawed frozen prepared pie shells all ready to bake.

Prepared pastry for a 9-inch pie
  shell
4 tablespoons butter
8 scallions, chopped
1 garlic clove, minced
1 (6-ounce) jar marinated arti-
  choke hearts, drained and
  coarsely chopped

2 cups shredded Gruyère cheese
  (about 8 ounces)
1¼ cups light cream
3 eggs
¼ teaspoon salt
¼ teaspoon pepper

1. Preheat oven to 400°F. Roll out pastry and line a 9-inch pie pan. Bake 10 minutes.

2. Reduce temperature to 375°. In a large skillet, melt butter over medium heat. Add scallions and garlic and cook until soft, 3 to 5 minutes. Add artichokes. Cook 1 minute. Spread on bottom of pie shell. Sprinkle with cheese.

3. In a medium bowl, beat together cream, eggs, salt, and pepper. Pour over scallion-cheese mixture.

4. Bake 35 minutes until golden and slightly puffy. Let stand 10 minutes before cutting. Serve warm or at room temperature.

285 🎔 Brioche Basket Filled with Brie

PREP: 30 minutes   RISE: 2 hours   CHILL: overnight
BAKE: 45 minutes   SERVES: 16 to 20

This gorgeous golden basket makes the perfect setting for a whole wheel of Brie. You could also use the inside of the bread to make tea sandwiches filled with your choice of savory spreads and set them back into the loaf. Put the lid back on your edible surprise package. Be sure to begin a day ahead, as the dough must be refrigerated overnight.

¾ cup sugar
¼ teaspoon salt
3 (¼-ounce) envelopes active dry
　yeast
5½ cups flour

2 sticks (8 ounces) butter
¾ cup milk
7 eggs
1 (2½-pound) wheel of Brie

1. In bowl of a large heavy-duty mixer fitted with paddle attachment, combine sugar, salt, yeast, and 2 cups flour. In a small saucepan, combine butter and milk. Cook over medium heat until butter is melted and mixture is lukewarm, 110° to 115°F. With mixer on low speed, add liquid to dry ingredients and beat until just combined. Increase speed to medium and beat 2 minutes. Gradually mix in 6 eggs, one at a time, and 1½ cups flour, beating 2 minutes. Add another 1½ cups flour and beat on low 5 minutes.

2. Place dough in a large greased bowl. Cover with a kitchen towel and let rise in a warm, draft-free place until doubled in bulk, about 1 hour. Punch dough down, then cover with plastic wrap and refrigerate overnight.

3. Next day, punch down dough, then turn out onto a floured work surface. Cover with an inverted bowl and let rest 15 minutes. Grease a 10-inch springform pan. Pat dough into pan, smoothing top. Cover with an inverted bowl and let rise until doubled in bulk, about 1 hour.

4. During last 15 minutes of rising, preheat oven to 325°F. Beat remaining egg with 2 teaspoons water to make a glaze. Brush glaze over dough. Bake 45 minutes, or until loaf is golden brown and bottom sounds hollow when tapped. Let cool on a wire rack.

5. When cool, slice off top and reserve for a lid. Hollow out bread with a fork, leaving a 1-inch border. Insert cheese into loaf and top with reserved lid. Cut into thin wedges to serve.

NOTE: If you do not own a heavy-duty mixer, use a wooden spoon to incorporate all the eggs into the dough. Gradually add enough flour to make a soft dough. Turn out dough onto a floured work surface and knead by hand until shiny and elastic, about 10 minutes.

CHRISTMAS EVE OPEN HOUSE

SERVES: 16

Wild Mushroom Lasagne
Baked Ziti with Ricotta Cheese and Broccoli
Green Bean Buffet Salad with Balsamic Vinaigrette
Quick Brie en Croûte
Baked Ham or Smoked Turkey
Assorted Olives and Nuts

Croquembouche

286 ⁉ Wild Mushroom Lasagne

PREP: 25 minutes   BAKE: 61 to 67 minutes   COOL: 10 minutes
SERVES: 8 to 10

If fresh wild mushrooms are unavailable, use a combination of fresh cultivated mushrooms and rehydrated dried wild mushrooms. Freshly grated imported Parmesan cheese will make all the difference in this recipe.

1 pound lasagne noodles
¼ cup olive oil
1 tablespoon finely chopped shallot or onion
2 pounds assorted fresh wild and/or cultivated mushrooms, thickly sliced
4 tablespoons butter
3 tablespoons flour
1 cup milk

1 cup chicken broth
2 tablespoons chopped parsley
1 tablespoon chopped fresh thyme or 1 teaspoon dried
¾ teaspoon salt
½ teaspoon pepper
¼ teaspoon grated nutmeg
1¼ cups grated Parmesan cheese (5 ounces)

1. In a large pot of boiling salted water, cook lasagne noodles, stirring several times in beginning to prevent noodles from sticking to each other, until tender but still firm, 12 to 15 minutes. Drain in a colander and cool under cold running water; drain again and set aside.

2. In a large skillet or flameproof casserole, heat olive oil over medium-high heat. Add shallot and mushrooms and cook, stirring occasionally, until mushroom liquid is exuded and then evaporates, about 10 minutes. Set aside.

3. In a large saucepan, melt butter over medium heat. Add flour and cook, stirring, 1 to 2 minutes without allowing flour to brown. Gradually whisk in milk and broth. Bring to a boil, whisking until smooth and thickened, 1 to 2 minutes. Reduce heat to low and cook, whisking occasionally, 2 to 3 minutes. Stir in cooked mushrooms as well as any cooking liquid remaining in skillet. Season with parsley, thyme, salt, pepper, and nutmeg.

4. To assemble lasagne, spread a thin layer of mushroom sauce on bottom of a greased 13- X 9-inch baking dish. Arrange a layer of lasagne noodles over sauce. Spread about ½ cup mushroom sauce over noodles and sprinkle evenly with about ¼ cup Parmesan cheese. Repeat layers of noodles, mushroom sauce, and Parmesan, ending with a top layer of sauce and Parmesan. (The recipe can be prepared up to this point a day in advance.)

5. To cook lasagne, preheat oven to 350°F. Cover dish with foil and bake 25 minutes (35 minutes if lasagne has been refrigerated). Uncover and bake 10 minutes longer, or until bubbly. Let stand 10 minutes before cutting into squares.

287 🕎 Baked Ziti with Ricotta Cheese and Broccoli

PREP: 40 minutes   BAKE: 20 to 30 minutes   SERVES: 6 to 8

This pretty red and green casserole can be assembled up to two days in advance, then popped into the oven about an hour before you're ready to serve.

1 pound ziti
1 head broccoli, cut into 1-inch florets
3 tablespoons olive oil
1 medium onion, chopped
1 garlic clove, crushed
1 (28-ounce) can Italian plum tomatoes, coarsely chopped, with their juice
1 (6-ounce) can tomato paste

1 cup dry red wine
1 teaspoon dried basil or oregano
¼ cup chopped parsley
½ teaspoon salt
¼ teaspoon black pepper
⅛ teaspoon crushed hot red pepper
½ pound ricotta cheese
⅛ teaspoon grated nutmeg
1 cup grated Parmesan cheese

1. In a large pot of boiling salted water, cook pasta until just tender, 8 to 10 minutes; drain well. Meanwhile, in a large saucepan of boiling water, cook broccoli until just tender, 2 to 3 minutes. Drain, rinse briefly under cold running water, and drain well.

2. In a large nonreactive saucepan or flameproof casserole, heat oil over medium heat. Add onion and cook until just beginning to turn golden, 3 to 5 minutes. Add garlic and cook 1 minute longer. Add tomatoes with their liquid, tomato paste, wine, basil, parsley, salt, black pepper, and hot pepper. Bring to a boil and reduce heat to medium-low. Partially cover and cook, stirring occasionally, until sauce thickens, 35 to 40 minutes.

3. Preheat oven to 375°F. Butter a 13- x 9- x 2-inch baking dish. Toss ziti with tomato sauce and transfer half to baking dish. In a medium bowl, blend together ricotta cheese, nutmeg, and ½ cup Parmesan cheese. Spread over ziti. Scatter broccoli florets over ricotta. Cover with remaining ziti. Sprinkle remaining Parmesan over top. Bake 20 to 30 minutes, or until hot and golden on top.

288 ¶ Green Bean Buffet Salad

PREP: 20 minutes   COOK: 3 to 5 minutes   SERVES: 12 to 16

The colors of Christmas and the flavors of Italy come together beautifully in this salad. For easy entertaining, the beans can be trimmed and cooked a day ahead and refrigerated; before assembling the salad, let them return to room temperature. To retain their bright green color, toss the beans with the dressing just before serving.

3 pounds fresh green beans
1 (7-ounce) jar roasted red
    peppers
½ medium sweet onion (yellow,
    white, or purple), sliced paper
    thin (optional)

Balsamic Vinaigrette (recipe
    follows)
½ cup oil-cured black olives, pitted

1. Trim ends off beans and, if large, cut in half. Bring a large pot of salted water to a boil over high heat. Add beans; when water returns to a rolling boil, cook 3 to 5 minutes, until crisp-tender. Drain beans in a colander and rinse under cold running water. Drain well. (If done in advance, wrap beans in a clean kitchen towel and store in a plastic bag in refrigerator up to 1 day.)

2. Drain roasted peppers well and cut into ¼-inch strips. In a large bowl, combine green beans, pepper strips, and onion slices. Toss lightly to mix.

3. Just before serving, pour vinaigrette over vegetables and toss until well coated. Transfer salad to a serving bowl or platter and scatter olives over top.

289 🎔 Balsamic Vinaigrette

PREP: 3 minutes   COOK: none   MAKES: 1 cup

Use as a marinade or on salads. A cup is a generous amount of dressing, which can be made ahead and used all at once or as you need it.

1 garlic clove, crushed
1 tablespoon Dijon mustard
¼ cup balsamic vinegar
¾ cup extra-virgin olive oil

¼ teaspoon salt
½ teaspoon pepper
1 tablespoon chopped parsley

Place all ingredients except parsley in a blender. Blend 2 minutes or until emulsified. Stir in parsley. Use immediately or refrigerate up to 3 days.

290 🕊 Quick Brie en Croûte

PREP: 20 minutes   BAKE: 30 minutes   SERVES: 6 to 8

Baking a wheel of Brie in a store-bought loaf of bread makes an original yet very practical presentation.

*1 small garlic clove, crushed
    through a press
2 tablespoons extra-virgin olive oil
1 (1- to 1½-pound) round loaf
    French or Italian bread*

*1 (8-ounce) wheel of Brie
1 tablespoon minced parsley*

1. Preheat oven to 350°F. In a small bowl, mix garlic in olive oil and set aside. Slice off top third of bread loaf. (Top of loaf can be reserved for other uses, such as bread crumbs, or sliced to serve with baked cheese.)

2. Using wheel of cheese as a guide, trace it on center of cut bread, then cut down as deep as the cheese is high (about 1 to 1½ inches). Scoop out center to fit cheese.

3. Cut ½-inch slices around edges of bread, taking care not to cut through bottom of loaf. Brush cut surfaces of bread with garlic oil and sprinkle with parsley. Without removing rind, insert cheese into center of loaf. Score top of cheese several times to ensure even baking.

4. Wrap loaf loosely in foil and place on a baking sheet. Bake until bread is lightly toasted and cheese begins to melt, about 30 minutes. As soon as bread is cool enough to handle, have guests pull off slices spread with melted cheese, using a small knife.

291 ✒ Croquembouche

PREP: 1¾ hours   COOK: 12 to 15 minutes   SERVES: 12 to 16

An edible edifice of cream puffs laced with caramel is awe-inspiring, to say the least. Although the puffs and pastry cream can be made well in advance, the final caramel glaze can be applied no more than four hours before serving, as it tends to soften quickly. Don't try to make this on a humid day—the caramel will soften and the puffs won't "crunch in the mouth" as the French name describes.

Pastry Cream (see page 182)　½ *cup light corn syrup*
Tiny Cream Puffs (see page 183)　¼ *cup water*
1 cup sugar

1. Using a pastry bag fitted with a ⅛-inch plain tip, pipe about 2 teaspoons pastry cream into each puff by pushing tip into a side of cream puff. Continue until all puffs are filled.

2. Make a caramel glaze by combining sugar, corn syrup, and water in a heavy medium saucepan. Cook over low heat, stirring occasionally, until sugar is dissolved, 5 to 6 minutes. Increase heat to medium-high and boil mixture, without stirring, until it is the color of honey, 7 to 9 minutes. (If syrup begins to color unevenly, swirl pot to redistribute heat but do not stir.) Stop cooking process by dipping bottom of pan in cold water.

3. On a 9-inch or larger serving platter, make a circle of 12 cream puffs for the base: Dip puffs, one at a time, into caramel, coating top half and 1 side. Arrange puffs on their sides, tops facing out and caramel-side up, until circle has been completed. Top with a second layer of 11 puffs, using caramel as glue. Continue building circular layers, using 1 puff less each time, until you have formed a cone about 10 layers high, ending with 3 puffs on top. (Depending upon how quickly you work, it may be necessary to gently reheat the caramel to keep it fluid. If caramel becomes too dark, make a new batch.)

4. Use tines of a fork to drizzle remaining caramel over cream puffs, creating a spun sugar effect. Croquembouche can be kept at cool room temperature up to 4 hours. Do not refrigerate. To serve, crack through caramel with a knife to detach cream puffs.

Pastry Cream

PREP: 15 minutes   COOK: 8 to 10 minutes   MAKES: 3 cups

This rich custard is an ideal filling for cream puffs, cakes, or tarts.

2 cups milk   *Dash salt*
6 egg yolks   *2 teaspoons vanilla extract*
½ cup sugar   *4 tablespoons butter, cut into bits*
¼ cup flour

1. In a medium saucepan, whisk together milk, egg yolks, sugar, flour, and salt until blended. Cook over medium-low heat, stirring, 8 to 10 minutes, or until medium thick. Remove from heat.

2. Stir in vanilla and butter until melted and incorporated. Strain into a medium bowl and place plastic wrap directly on surface of pastry cream to prevent a skin from forming. Use tip of knife to poke 6 to 8 slits in plastic to allow escape of steam. Let cool. If made in advance, refrigerate up to 3 days.

Tiny Cream Puffs

PREP: 45 minutes   COOK: 22 to 23 minutes   MAKES: about 75

These bite-size puffs for croquembouche can also be filled with any number of sweet or savory fillings. After baking, they freeze beautifully. If you do not have a food processor, beat in the eggs one at a time with a wooden spoon, making sure that each is fully incorporated before adding the next.

2 sticks (8 ounces) butter, cut into tablespoons	1 teaspoon salt
1 teaspoon sugar	2 cups flour
	8 eggs

1. Preheat oven to 400°F. Line 2 baking sheets with parchment paper. In a large saucepan, combine butter, sugar, and salt with 2 cups water. Bring to a boil over medium heat, adjusting heat as necessary so butter is fully melted when mixture boils. Reduce heat to low and add flour all at once, beating vigorously with a wooden spoon until dough is well blended and forms a ball, leaving a film on bottom and sides of pan, 2 to 3 minutes. Remove from heat and let cool 5 minutes.

2. Transfer half of dough to a food processor and process until broken into bits, 10 to 15 seconds. Add 4 eggs and process until smooth and shiny, 30 to 45 seconds. Remove from processor. Repeat procedure, using second half of dough and remaining 4 eggs.

3. Using 2 spoons or a pastry bag fitted with a plain ½-inch tip, drop small mounds of dough (about 1 inch in diameter) on baking sheets. Use a damp brush or your fingertip to smooth tops.

4. Bake for 10 minutes. Reduce oven temperature to 350° and continue baking until puffed and golden brown, about 10 minutes. Let cool on a rack. (If made in advance, store airtight up to 1 day at room temperature. Freeze for longer storage. Before serving, recrisp puffs 5 to 10 minutes in a 400° oven.)

CHILDREN'S CHRISTMAS TABLE

SERVES: 8 TO 10

Christmas Pizza Bites

Crown Roast of Frankfurters with Baked Beans
Cheddar Corn Casserole with Red and Green Peppers
Sweet Potato Crunch

Almond Butter Cookies
Ice cream

292 ♦ Christmas Pizza Bites

PREP: 15 minutes   COOK: 3 to 4 minutes   MAKES: 36

Kids love pizza, any time of year. With this recipe you can turn easy pita pizzas into bite-size wedges. You'll have more than enough to go around.

3 (7-inch) wheat pita breads
¾ cup pasta, spaghetti, or pizza sauce
10 ounces shredded Monterey Jack or mozzarella cheese
½ cup diced red and green bell pepper

1. Carefully tear pita breads around edges and open up so that each forms 2 thin rounds. There will be 6 rounds.
2. Spread 2 tablespoons pasta sauce over each round. Sprinkle cheese over sauce, dividing evenly. Decorate pizzas with bits of pepper for holiday color.
3. Preheat broiler. Broil pizzas 4 to 6 inches from heat for 3 to 4 minutes, until cheese is melted and pizza is bubbling hot. Let cool slightly and cut each round into wedges to serve.

293 ✍ Crown Roast of Frankfurters with Baked Beans

PREP: 15 minutes   BAKE: 25 minutes   SERVES: 8 to 10

Children seem to love high drama at their celebrations, so this fanciful presentation of favorite foods is sure to please. Use the longer bun-size frankfurters if you can find them. To form the crown, you'll need seven long toothpicks and a piece of white kitchen string.

3 (16-ounce) cans baked beans
½ cup finely chopped onion
⅓ cup packed dark brown sugar

2 teaspoons Dijon mustard
3 (12-ounce) packages frank-
furters (about 21)

1. Preheat oven to 400°F. In a medium saucepan, combine baked beans, onion, brown sugar, and mustard. Stir until well mixed. Cook over medium heat, stirring occasionally, until beans are hot, 10 to 15 minutes.

2. Meanwhile, rinse frankfurters and blot dry with paper towels. Spear 3 frankfurters together by pushing a toothpick horizontally through upper third of franks. Repeat with remaining frankfurters.

3. Place a 6-inch-tall 1½- to 2-quart baking dish about 4½ inches in diameter (such as a bean pot) on an ovenproof serving platter. Lean frankfurters, skewered ends up, around outside edge of bean pot. Tie a piece of kitchen string around center of franks to secure them in a circle. Remove toothpicks.

4. Transfer hot beans from saucepan to pot in center of franks and place platter and all in oven. Bake until frankfurters are golden brown and beans are bubbly, about 25 minutes. To serve, spoon beans directly from pot and use tongs to remove frankfurters.

294 🖤 Cheddar Corn Casserole with Red and Green Peppers

PREP: 10 minutes   BAKE: 30 to 35 minutes   SERVES: 8 to 10

1 stick (4 ounces) butter, melted
1 large onion, chopped
½ medium green bell pepper, diced
½ medium red bell pepper, diced
1 garlic clove, minced
3 eggs
1 cup sour cream

1 (16-ounce) can cream-style corn
⅓ cup yellow cornmeal
¼ teaspoon salt
¼ teaspoon pepper
1¼ cups shredded Cheddar cheese
   (5 ounces)

1. Preheat oven to 350°F. In a medium skillet, heat 2 table-spoons butter over medium heat. Add onion and green and red peppers and cook, stirring occasionally, until soft, 3 to 5 minutes. Add garlic and cook 1 to 2 minutes. Remove from heat and set aside.

2. In a large bowl, combine remaining 6 tablespoons butter, eggs, and sour cream. Whisk until smooth. Mix in corn, cornmeal, salt, and pepper. Stir in cheese and cooked onion, peppers, and garlic. Turn into a greased 2-quart casserole.

3. Bake 30 to 35 minutes, until puffed, golden, and set in center.

295 🕭 Sweet Potato Crunch

PREP: 45 minutes   BAKE: 15 to 20 minutes   SERVES: 8 to 10

3 pounds sweet potatoes
1 stick (4 ounces) unsalted butter,
    melted
½ cup packed brown sugar

¼ cup orange juice
1½ teaspoons cinnamon
¼ teaspoon salt
1½ cups graham cracker crumbs

1. In a pot of boiling water, cook sweet potatoes until tender, 35 to 40 minutes; drain. As soon as they are cool enough to handle, peel.

2. Preheat oven to 400°F. In a large bowl, mash sweet potatoes. Add 4 tablespoons butter, brown sugar, orange juice, cinnamon, and salt and mix until smooth.

3. In another bowl, combine graham cracker crumbs and remaining 4 tablespoons butter.

4. Spread sweet potato mixture in a greased 9-inch square baking pan. Top with buttered crumbs. Bake until hot and bubbly, 15 to 20 minutes.

296 ❧ Almond Butter Cookies

PREP: 20 minutes   BAKE: 7 to 8 minutes per batch
MAKES: about 120

These light and flaky rolled cookies, with their rich almond flavor, have a creamy white color that makes them perfect for shaping and decorating. Poke a hole through one side, so that they can be hung on the Christmas tree. This cookie dough does not expand when baked, so you can make the hole the size of your ribbon or string.

4 ounces almond paste
1 (16-ounce) box powdered sugar
5 sticks (1¼ pounds) unsalted
   butter, softened
3 eggs
½ cup milk

2 teaspoons vanilla extract
8 cups cake flour
1 teaspoon salt
All-purpose flour
Decorating Icing (recipe follows)

1. Preheat oven to 375°F. Grease 4 large cookie sheets.
2. In a large bowl, crumble almond paste into powdered sugar with your hands until almond paste is almost powdery. Beat in butter with an electric mixer until smooth. Add eggs, one at a time, beating in thoroughly after each addition. Add milk and vanilla and beat well. Mix in cake flour and salt until a soft pliable dough forms.
3. Take a large handful of dough and knead, using all-purpose flour on your hands and on the table, until smooth. Shape into a thick circle and roll out ⅛ inch thick, making sure to use plenty of flour to prevent sticking. Dip cookie cutters in flour and cut out as many cookies as possible. Arrange cookies about ½ inch apart on cookie sheets. Knead scraps back into remaining dough and repeat until finished.
4. Bake cookies in batches 7 to 8 minutes, or until cookie looks firm and bottom is lightly browned. Do not overbake. Immediately transfer cookies to racks and let cool completely. Decorate as desired before serving.

297 🖉 Decorating Icing

PREP: 5 to 30 minutes   COOK: none   MAKES: 1 cup

This icing is good for decorating Christmas cookies, and it contains no uncooked egg white, so it is perfectly safe. Separate icing into bowls before adding food coloring to make different colors. While a paper cone can be used, a pastry bag is by far the simplest way to pipe this icing. If you do not have one, a kitchen equipment shop will offer various models. Buy a small one and a few different pastry tips.

1 cup powdered sugar   *Food coloring*
4 teaspoons condensed milk

In a medium bowl, combine powdered sugar and condensed milk. Stir until a soft smooth paste forms. Separate icing into small bowls and stir a drop or two of coloring into each, depending on shade you want. Use at once, before icing sets.

VICTORIAN CHRISTMAS DINNER

SERVES: 6 TO 8

Claret Punch
Herbed Cheddar Wafers

Oyster Stew

Roast Goose with Sage and Onion Stuffing
Lemony Apple Compote
Mashed Rutabagas and Potatoes
Braised Red Cabbage
Buttered peas

Plum Pudding with Brandy Hard Sauce

298 🎵 Claret Punch

PREP: 5 minutes   STAND: 10 minutes   COOK: none
MAKES: about 22 (4-ounce) servings

Grand Marnier, Cointreau, Curaçao, or any other orange-flavored liqueur can be substituted for the triple sec here.

4 juice oranges
¼ cup triple sec
½ cup blackberry-flavored brandy
2 (750-ml) bottles dry red wine,
  chilled

1 liter seltzer, chilled
½ cup lemon juice
Ice

1. Slice oranges and place in a large punch bowl. Sprinkle triple sec and blackberry-flavored brandy over oranges. Let orange slices macerate in liquor 10 to 15 minutes.

2. Add red wine, seltzer, and lemon juice to punch bowl. Stir gently and add a large block of ice. Ladle into punch cups.

299 ❧ Herbed Cheddar Wafers

PREP: 10 minutes   CHILL: 1 hour   COOK: 10 to 12 minutes
MAKES: 48

A favorite buttery cheese biscuit is enhanced by the pungent flavor of rosemary.

1 stick (4 ounces) butter, softened
2 cups shredded sharp Cheddar
   cheese (about 8 ounces)
1 cup flour

¼ teaspoon salt
⅛ teaspoon cayenne
1 tablespoon chopped fresh rosemary or 1 teaspoon dried

1. Preheat oven to 425°F. In a medium bowl or in a food processor, blend butter and cheese until well mixed. Mix in flour, salt, cayenne, and rosemary until well blended.
2. Divide dough into 3 equal portions. Form each piece into a cylinder 1 inch in diameter. Wrap tightly in plastic wrap, twisting ends to seal. Refrigerate or freeze until firm, about 1 hour.
3. Remove plastic wrap and slice dough ⅛ inch thick. Arrange slices in a single layer on an ungreased baking sheet and bake 10 to 12 minutes, or until wafers are firm and just barely browned at edges. Transfer to a rack and let cool. Store airtight up to 4 days or freeze.

300 🐚 Oyster Stew

PREP: 5 minutes   COOK: 5 minutes   SERVES: 6 to 8

3 tablespoons unsalted butter
2 pints shucked oysters, liquor
  reserved and strained
½ teaspoon salt
¼ teaspoon ground mace

¼ teaspoon white pepper
Pinch cayenne
2 cups milk
2 cups light cream

1. In large heavy saucepan, melt butter over medium-low heat. Add oysters and their liquor. Season with salt, mace, white pepper, and cayenne. Cook oysters just until they plump up and their edges start to curl, about 5 minutes.

2. Meanwhile, in another saucepan, combine milk and cream. Cook over medium heat until hot but not boiling. Be careful not to scorch it. Add hot milk mixture to cooked oysters, mix well, and serve at once in heated bowls.

301 ✒ Roast Goose with Sage and Onion Stuffing

PREP: 40 minutes   ROAST: about 3 hours   SERVES: 6 to 8

1 (10- to 12-pound) goose
1½ teaspoons salt
3 tablespoons butter
4 medium onions, coarsely
　chopped
1 goose liver

4 cups (1-inch) bread cubes
1½ teaspoons dried sage
½ teaspoon salt
½ teaspoon pepper
½ cup dry white wine
1 egg, lightly beaten

1. Preheat oven to 425°F. Rinse goose inside and out; drain well. Rub inside of goose with salt. Set aside.

2. In a large saucepan or flameproof casserole, melt 2 tablespoons butter over medium heat. Add onions and cook, stirring occasionally, until soft and translucent, about 7 minutes. Remove onions to a large mixing bowl.

3. Melt remaining 1 tablespoon butter in same pan over moderately high heat. Add goose liver and cook until just cooked through but not dry, about 4 minutes on each side. Chop liver and add it and butter from saucepan to onions. Add bread, sage, salt, pepper, wine, and egg. Toss all together lightly.

3. Remove wing tips from goose. (These and remaining giblets can be browned and cooked in a little water to make stock for gravy.) Stuff both neck and large cavity of goose. Sew or skewer vent closed. Lightly prick skin of thighs, back, and lower breast of goose.

4. Put goose, breast side up, in a roasting pan. Roast in preheated oven 30 minutes. Reduce oven temperature to 350°, turn goose on its side, and roast 1 hour, basting with 2 to 3 tablespoons hot water every 20 minutes. Turn goose onto its other side and roast, basting, 1 hour. Finally, turn breast side up once more and roast 30 minutes, or until goose is browned all over and drumsticks feel quite tender.

4. Transfer goose to a serving platter and let stand 10 minutes before carving. Remove fat from roasting pan and use brown pan drippings to make gravy, if desired.

302 ﴾﴿ Lemony Apple Compote

PREP: 10 minutes   COOK: 20 to 25 minutes   SERVES: 6 to 8

1 small lemon
6 medium apples, peeled, cored,
  and cut into ½-inch dice

1½ cups sugar
¼ teaspoon ground mace

1. Grate colored zest from lemon, avoiding bitter white pith. Set aside. Squeeze lemon juice into a medium bowl. Add apples to bowl and toss with juice.

2. In a heavy medium saucepan, combine sugar and ¾ cup water. Bring to a boil over medium heat, stirring once or twice. Reduce heat to medium–low, add lemon zest, apples, and lemon juice.

3. Cook, stirring occasionally, 10 minutes. Add mace and cook 10 to 15 minutes, or until apples are translucent and syrup has nearly boiled away. Serve warm.

303 ﴾﴿ Mashed Rutabagas and Potatoes

PREP: 15 minutes   COOK: 30 minutes   SERVES: 6 to 8

In England, rutabagas or yellow turnips are called "swedes," supposedly after their country of origin, which probably was, in fact, Russia. Botanists believe the rutabaga is a spontaneous hybrid between the cabbage and the turnip. Combining this highly flavored root with potatoes produces a smooth, mellow mixture that's just perfect for midwinter feasting.

2½ pounds rutabaga, peeled and
  cut into 2-inch pieces
1½ teaspoons salt
2 pounds potatoes (4 or
  5 medium), peeled and
  cut into 2-inch cubes

2 tablespoons butter
½ cup milk
¼ teaspoon pepper
¼ teaspoon grated nutmeg
2 teaspoons chopped parsley

1. Put rutabaga in a heavy pot with 1½ cups water and salt. Bring water to a boil, cover pot tightly, and cook rutabaga over medium-low heat until tender, about 30 minutes. Drain in a colander. Puree rutabaga in a food processor or mash as smoothly as possible.

2. While the rutabaga is cooking, put potatoes into a large saucepan of lightly salted boiling water and cook until tender, 20 to 25 minutes. Drain potatoes and let them dry for a few minutes. Mash potatoes or put them through a ricer or food mill.

3. In a large bowl, combine mashed potatoes with pureed rutabaga and mix well. Beat in butter, milk, pepper, and nutmeg. Season with additional salt to taste. If necessary, reheat preferably in a microwave. Serve hot, garnished with chopped parsley.

304 ⟨ℕ Braised Red Cabbage

PREP: 5 minutes   COOK: 40 minutes   SERVES: 6 to 8

2 tablespoons unsalted butter
6 ounces Canadian bacon, cut
   into ¼-inch dice
1 large head red cabbage
   (3½ pounds) quartered, cored,
   and cut into ¼-inch slices
2 cups homemade unsalted
   chicken stock or reduced-
   sodium canned broth

½ cup red wine vinegar
1 tablespoon sugar
1 teaspoon salt
½ teaspoon pepper

1. In a large nonreactive flameproof casserole, melt butter over medium-low heat. Add Canadian bacon and cook until pieces begin to brown.

2. Add red cabbage, chicken stock, vinegar, sugar, and salt. Cover and cook over medium-low heat until cabbage is tender, about 30 minutes. Remove cover, increase heat to medium-high, and cook, stirring frequently, until liquid is reduced to a light sauce. Season with pepper and additional salt to taste.

305 🎄 Buttered Peas

Green peas were a favorite Christmas dish long before the invention of tin cans and freezers. Cookbooks printed in England and America during the 1700s included instructions on how to keep green peas until Christmas. After blanching or salting, the peas were packed in jars; then the jars were filled with melted fat and sealed. Early on, the containers that held the peas were earthenware, with seals made of thin leather. Later, glass jars were stoppered with corks, which were then dipped in melted rosin.

306 🎄 Plum Pudding

PREP: 20 minutes   STAND: several hours or overnight
COOK: 3 to 4 hours   SERVES: 8

This updated version of plum pudding replaces traditional beef suet with butter. It's more convenient and yields a lighter result. An eight-cup pudding mold is ideal for this recipe, but two coffee cans and aluminum foil will do just fine. The "plums" in this dessert are actually raisins. If possible, make plum puddings three weeks to a month before Christmas and let them age so their flavors will develop and mellow. To do so, see the note at the end of the recipe.

4 ounces candied citrus peel, finely chopped
½ cup walnuts, finely chopped
1 (15-ounce) box raisins
¾ cup sweet cider
¾ cup brandy
1 cup flour
1 cup fine bread crumbs
1 teaspoon cinnamon

½ teaspoon ground ginger
½ teaspoon grated nutmeg
¼ teaspoon ground cloves
1 stick (4 ounces) unsalted butter, softened
½ cup packed brown sugar
3 eggs
Brandy Hard Sauce (recipe follows)

1. In a glass or ceramic bowl, combine candied peel, walnuts, raisins, cider, and ¼ cup brandy. Cover and let stand several hours or overnight, stirring occasionally.

2. In a medium bowl, combine flour, bread crumbs, cinnamon, ginger, nutmeg, and cloves. Stir or whisk gently to mix well. In a large bowl, beat together butter and brown sugar until light and fluffy. Beat in eggs one at a time. Stir in flour mixture to make a thick batter. Add brandied fruit and walnuts and mix well.

3. Spoon batter into a well-greased 8-cup mold or 2 well-greased 4-cup molds. Molds should be no more than three-fourths full. Cover and place in a large pot. Fill pot with enough water to reach three-fourths of the way up sides of mold. Bring water to a boil, reduce heat to medium-low, cover tightly, and steam pudding, 4 hours for large mold and 3 hours for 2 smaller molds. Check water level occasionally.

4. Remove pudding mold from water and let pudding cool in mold for a few minutes, then turn out onto a serving plate. Douse with ¼ or ½ cup of brandy, depending on size of pudding, and carefully ignite with a match. Serve with Brandy Hard Sauce as soon as flames subside.

NOTE: If made ahead, let the pudding cool completely before turning it out. Wrap in 2 or 3 thicknesses of cheesecloth. Douse cloth with additional brandy—about ⅓ cup for a large pudding. Seal each pudding in a plastic bag with a tie, then place in a closed container in a cool place.

When ready to serve pudding, remove cheesecloth, sprinkle pudding with ¼ cup brandy and wrap tightly in aluminum foil. Place pudding in a 350°F oven for about 30 minutes. Flame with another ¼ cup brandy and serve with Brandy Hard Sauce.

307 🎄 Brandy Hard Sauce

PREP: 3 minutes   COOK: none   SERVES: 8

By custom, plum pudding is served with a sauce, and this is one
of the most traditional.

1 stick (4 ounces) unsalted butter,   *1½ cups powdered sugar*
    softened   *⅓ cup brandy*

Beat butter with an electric mixer or, by hand, with a whisk
until fluffy. Gradually beat in sugar, then brandy, 1 tablespoon at
a time, to make a sauce with consistency of very heavy cream.

A TRADITIONAL CHRISTMAS DINNER

SERVES: 8

Bay Scallop Bisque

Roast Turkey with Chicken Sausage Stuffing
Sweet Potatoes with Dried Peaches and Apricots
Pureed Turnips with Parmesan Cheese
Wild rice
Buttered broccoli
Cranberry Bread

Bûche de Noël

308 🐚 Bay Scallop Bisque

PREP: 10 minutes   COOK: 13 to 20 minutes   SERVES: 6 to 8

4 tablespoons butter
6 large shallots, minced
1 cup dry white wine
2 cups half-and-half
1 pound bay scallops

1 tablespoon chopped fresh tar-
ragon or 1 teaspoon dried
½ teaspoon salt
¼ teaspoon white pepper

1. In a large nonreactive saucepan, melt butter over low heat. Add shallots and cook until softened but not browned, 3 to 5 minutes. Stir in wine and increase heat to medium-high. Boil until liquid is reduced to about 2 tablespoons, 7 to 10 minutes.

2. Whisk in half-and-half and bring to a boil. Reduce heat to low and stir in scallops. Cook until scallops are just cooked through and opaque in center, 3 to 5 minutes. Season with tarragon, salt, and pepper. Serve warm.

309 🐦 Roast Turkey with Chicken Sausage Stuffing

PREP: 30 minutes   ROAST: 3½ to 4 hours   SERVES: 8

An alternative to turkey is small game hens. The amount of stuffing in this recipe will fill six Cornish game hens. Bake the stuffed birds for about an hour to an hour and a quarter.

4 tablespoons vegetable oil
1 pound chicken or turkey
    sausage, removed from casing
1 large onion, chopped
2 celery ribs, chopped
3 cups cubed stale pumpernickel
    bread
2 large eggs

1 (10- to 12-pound) turkey,
    thawed if frozen
1 teaspoon sage
1 teaspoon paprika
½ teaspoon salt
¼ teaspoon pepper
1 cup chicken broth
1 cup dry white wine

1. In a large skillet, heat 2 tablespoons oil over medium heat. Add sausage and cook, breaking up pieces with a fork until lightly browned and cooked through, 5 to 7 minutes. Remove to a large bowl and set aside. In same pan, heat remaining 2 tablespoons oil. Add onion and celery and cook until soft, 3 to 5 minutes. Remove to bowl with sausage. Let cool slightly.

2. Add bread cubes and eggs; mix well. Preheat oven to 350°F. Remove giblets and neck from turkey. (Use for stock or refrigerate for another use.) Rinse turkey inside and out; pat dry. Season skin of turkey with sage, paprika, salt, and pepper. Stuff loosely with filling.

3. Place turkey, breast side up, in a large roasting pan. Pour chicken broth and wine around turkey. Roast until tender and juices run clear when thigh is pricked with a fork, 3½ to 4 hours, basting every 30 minutes.

310 ❧ Sweet Potatoes with Dried Peaches and Apricots

PREP: 10 minutes   COOK: 45 minutes   SERVES: 8

1 (8-ounce) can mandarin
    orange slices, liquid reserved
1 cup apricot nectar
½ pound dried apricots
½ pound dried peaches
2 (16-ounce) cans sweet potatoes,
    drained and sliced

1 stick (4 ounces) unsalted butter,
    melted
2 tablespoons dark or amber rum
1 teaspoon grated orange zest
¾ cup packed brown sugar

1. In a medium saucepan, combine reserved mandarin orange liquid, apricot nectar, and 1 cup water. Bring to boil. Add dried apricots and peaches. Reduce heat to low and simmer until tender, about 20 minutes. Remove fruit to a bowl; reserve cooking liquid.

2. Preheat oven to 350°F. In a 2-quart baking dish, layer half of sliced potatoes and then half of dried fruit. Add all of mandarin orange slices. Top with layers of remaining sweet potatoes and dried fruit.

3. In a bowl, whisk together melted butter, rum, orange zest, and reserved cooking liquid. Pour over potato-fruit mixture. Sprinkle brown sugar over top.

4. Bake 25 minutes, or until hot and bubbly.

311 🐦 Pureed Turnips with Parmesan Cheese

PREP: 10 minutes   COOK: 10 minutes   SERVES: 8

The turnip, that much misunderstood winter vegetable, gains mainstream popularity thanks to a bit of cream and cheese. Try this as a substitute for mashed potatoes.

2 pounds white turnips, peeled
*   and cut into 1-inch pieces*
¼ cup heavy cream
¼ cup grated Parmesan cheese

2 tablespoons butter, softened
½ teaspoon salt
¼ teaspoon white pepper

1. Cook turnips in a large saucepan of boiling salted water until tender, about 10 minutes. Drain in a colander.

2. In a food processor, finely chop one-third of turnips. Add remaining turnips in 2 batches, processing until a coarse paste is formed. Add cream, Parmesan cheese, butter, salt, and pepper and process until smooth.

3. Serve immediately, or cover and refrigerate up to 2 days. Reheat in a microwave or double boiler before serving.

312 🌿 Cranberry Bread

PREP: 10 minutes   BAKE: 50 to 55 minutes   SERVES: 8

1 cup walnuts (about 4 ounces)
1 stick (4 ounces) unsalted butter, melted
1 cup sugar
1 egg
1 cup orange juice

3 cups flour
1 tablespoon baking powder
½ teaspoon grated orange zest
¼ teaspoon salt
1 cup fresh or frozen cranberries

1. Preheat oven to 350°F. Grease a 9- X 5- X 3-inch loaf pan. Place nuts on a baking sheet and toast in oven until very lightly browned and fragrant, about 5 minutes. Leave oven on. Coarsely chop nuts and set aside.

2. In a large bowl, using a hand-held electric mixer, beat butter and sugar until light and fluffy. Add egg. Beat 1 minute. Gradually beat in juice. Add flour, baking powder, orange zest, and salt. Mix until just blended. Stir in cranberries and toasted walnuts. Spread batter into pan.

3. Bake until top of loaf is golden and a toothpick inserted in center comes out clean, 50 to 55 minutes. Let set in pan for 10 minutes, then unmold onto a wire rack and let cool completely.

313 🎄 Bûche de Noël

The bakers of Paris, ever imaginative, created an edible log, the Bûche de Noël, as a way for city dwellers to partake in the holiday tradition of the yule log.

Sponge Cake

PREP: 10 minutes   BAKE: 12 to 15 minutes   SERVES: 16

⅓ cup cake flour
⅓ cup cornstarch
5 eggs, separated
¼ teaspoon cream of tartar
½ cup sugar

1 teaspoon vanilla extract
Chocolate Butter Cream (recipe
    follows)
Meringue Mushrooms
    (see page 206)

1. Preheat oven to 375°F. Butter a rimmed 10- X 15-inch cookie sheet and line with parchment paper. Sift together flour and cornstarch.

2. In a large bowl, using a hand-held electric mixer, beat egg whites on medium speed until soft peaks form. Increase speed to high. Add cream of tartar and gradually add ¼ cup sugar. Beat until whites are stiff and shiny; set aside.

3. In another bowl, using a hand-held electric mixer, beat yolks on high speed with remaining ¼ cup sugar and vanilla until mixture is thick, pale yellow, and forms a ribbon when beaters are lifted. Fold in half of beaten egg whites. Add sifted flour and cornstarch. Then fold in remaining egg whites.

4. Spread batter into pan and smooth top. Bake 12 to 15 minutes, or until cake is springy to touch. Let cool in pan on a wire rack for 10 to 15 minutes. Cover with a slightly dampened kitchen towel and invert onto another cookie sheet. Peel parchment off cake. Roll up from a long side, cover with kitchen towel, and let cool completely. Meanwhile, make butter cream frosting.

5. Unroll cake and spread with about half of butter cream. Roll again tightly from a long side and place, seam side down, on a plate. Cut off a 2-inch piece, on the diagonal, from each end of roll for branches. Attach to log with toothpicks. Cover log with remaining butter cream. Score with a fork to resemble bark. While frosting is soft, attach meringue mushrooms or place around log. To serve, cut log into ½-inch slices.

Chocolate Butter Cream

PREP: 10 minutes   COOK: 8 to 10 minutes
MAKES: about 2½ cups

½ cup sugar
4 egg yolks
2 sticks (8 ounces) unsalted but-
    ter, cut into pieces, softened

⅔ cup chocolate chips (4 ounces),
    melted

1. In a small saucepan, over medium heat, cook sugar and ¼ cup water, stirring just until sugar dissolves. Bring to a boil without stirring and cook until syrup reaches soft ball stage, 238°F on a candy thermometer. This will take 8 to 10 minutes.

2. In a large bowl, using a hand-held electric mixer, beat egg yolks on medium speed until thick and pale yellow. Gradually beat in hot syrup in a thin stream, being careful not to let liquid fall on sides of bowl or beaters. Beat until cool. Add butter, a few pieces at a time, until incorporated. Blend in chocolate.

Meringue Mushrooms

PREP: 5 minutes   COOK: 1⅔ to 1¾ hours   MAKES: 20

2 egg whites
¼ teaspoon cream of tartar
¼ cup sugar
1 ounce sweet or semisweet choco-
*   late, melted*

1 tablespoon unsweetened cocoa
*   powder*

1. Preheat oven to 250°F. In a medium mixing bowl, using a hand-held electric mixer, beat egg whites on medium speed until soft peaks form. Increase speed to high. Add cream of tartar. Gradually add sugar. Beat until whites are stiff and shiny.

2. Line a cookie sheet with parchment paper. Fit a pastry bag with a ½-inch plain tip and fill with meringue. Pipe out meringue in mounds for caps. Pipe out stems separately.

3. Bake 40 to 45 minutes until firm. Turn oven off. Leave pan in oven 1 hour to dry.

4. With tip of a knife, hollow out caps slightly. Attach stems to caps with a dab of melted chocolate. Let stand until set. Dust caps lightly with cocoa powder.

IRISH HUNT BREAKFAST

SERVES: 8 TO 10

Citrus Fizz

Irish Soda Bread
Honey Butter

Gratin of Eggs with Canadian Bacon and Blarney Cheese
Broccoli with Mustard Vinaigrette

Gingerbread Muffins
Poached Pears with Irish Whiskey Sauce

314   Citrus Fizz

PREP: 2 minutes   COOK: none   SERVES: 8 to 10

This nonalcoholic sparkler is as festive as it is refreshing. Prepare pitchers of juice and chill bottles of soda in advance so it can be assembled easily.

6 cups fresh orange or grapefruit   *2 cups club soda*
   juice, chilled

    Combine juice and soda in a glass pitcher. Stir briefly to blend. Pour into goblets and serve immediately.

315 ⚜ Irish Soda Bread

PREP: 15 minutes   BAKE: 1 hour   COOL: 30 minutes
MAKES: 1 loaf

Maggie Doherty has been making this slightly sweet bread for friends and family for over fifty years, and people still ask for the recipe. While it is traditional for St. Patrick's Day, it is wonderful for brunch any day of the year, and certainly on Christmas.

4 cups flour
1 cup dark raisins
1 cup golden raisins
¼ cup sugar
1 teaspoon baking soda

1 teaspoon salt
2 cups buttermilk
1 egg
Honey Butter (recipe follows)

1. Preheat oven to 375°F. Generously grease a 9-inch round cake pan.
2. In a large bowl, combine flour, dark raisins, golden raisins, sugar, baking soda, and salt. Stir until well mixed. Make a well in center.
3. In a medium bowl, combine buttermilk and egg. Beat until well blended. Pour into well in flour mixture and stir to mix thoroughly. Do this with your hands, as dough is quite sticky.
4. Mound dough into prepared pan. Moisten hands lightly to smooth top. Score a cross on top of loaf to ensure even baking.
5. Bake 1 hour, or until a golden crust forms and loaf sounds hollow when tapped. Let cool at least 30 minutes. Serve warm or at room temperature with Honey Butter.

316 ⚜ Honey Butter

PREP: 5 minutes   COOK: none   MAKES: about 1 cup

2 sticks (8 ounces) butter, softened   ½ to ⅔ cup honey, to taste

1. In a food processor or blender, combine butter and honey and process until well blended. Pack into crocks, or refrigerate until barely firm and form into 2 to 4 cylinders on plastic wrap; roll up and twist ends to seal.

2. Refrigerate up to 10 days; freeze for longer storage.

317 ⁀ Gratin of Eggs with Canadian Bacon and Blarney Cheese

PREP: 15 minutes   COOK: 16 to 18 minutes   SERVES: 8 to 10

As you might expect, Blarney cheese comes from Ireland. If unavailable, substitute another flavorful melting cheese, such as Emmenthal or Gruyère.

¾ pound Canadian bacon, sliced
½ pound Blarney or Swiss cheese, thinly sliced or shredded
12 eggs
½ teaspoon salt
¼ teaspoon pepper
1 cup heavy cream
½ cup grated Parmesan cheese (2 ounces)
2 tablespoons freshly chopped chives
Paprika

1. Line a well-greased ovenproof, shallow 2½-quart baking dish with an even layer of Canadian bacon. Top with a layer of cheese. (If made in advance, cover tightly with plastic wrap and refrigerate up to 2 days.) Preheat oven to 375°F.

2. Break eggs in a single layer over surface of cheese. Season with salt and pepper. Drizzle cream over eggs, covering whites and allowing yolks to barely peek through. Bake 8 minutes.

3. Sprinkle evenly with Parmesan cheese and continue baking 8 to 10 minutes longer, until yolks are almost set to your liking. (Eggs will continue to cook after being removed from oven.) Top with chives and/or paprika. Cut into squares and serve warm.

318 🎄 Broccoli with Mustard Vinaigrette

PREP: 15 minutes   COOK: 2 to 3 minutes   SERVES: 8 to 10

A crisp green broccoli salad brightens up any holiday buffet.

*2 bunches fresh broccoli, cut into
   bite-size pieces (about
   2 pounds)*
2 tablespoons white wine vinegar
1 tablespoon Dijon mustard

*1 garlic clove, crushed through a
   press*
½ teaspoon salt
¼ teaspoon pepper
½ cup extra-virgin olive oil

1. In a large pot of boiling salted water, cook broccoli until crisp-tender, 2 to 3 minutes. Drain in a colander and rinse under cold running water until cool. Drain well. If made in advance, cover with plastic wrap and refrigerate up to 24 hours.

2. In a small bowl, combine vinegar, mustard, garlic, salt, and pepper until well blended. Whisk in olive oil until well blended.

3. Arrange broccoli on a serving platter. Just before serving, drizzle vinaigrette over broccoli.

319 🐿 Gingerbread Muffins

PREP: 30 minutes   CHILL: 24 hours   BAKE: 20 to 25 minutes
MAKES: 24

Make the batter one or two days in advance and bake these cakelike muffins Christmas morning, so your home is filled with the fragrance of gingerbread.

1 teaspoon baking soda
½ cup buttermilk
¾ cup solid vegetable shortening
½ cup granulated sugar
½ cup packed dark brown sugar
2 eggs

½ cup dark corn syrup
2 cups flour
2 teaspoons ground ginger
1½ teaspoons cinnamon
½ teaspoon ground allspice
½ teaspoon ground cloves

1. In a small bowl, dissolve baking soda in buttermilk, stirring to blend.

2. Using an electric mixer set at medium speed, beat shortening, granulated sugar, and brown sugar together until light and fluffy, about 5 minutes. With machine on, add eggs, one at a time, until well blended. Mix in corn syrup.

3. In a medium bowl or on a sheet of wax paper, sift together flour, ginger, cinnamon, allspice, and cloves. Add to butter mixture, alternating with buttermilk mixture, beating well after each addition, until well blended. Cover and refrigerate 24 hours or as long as 2 days.

4. Preheat oven to 350°F. Grease 24 muffin cups or line with paper baking cups. Spoon batter into muffin cups, filling about three-fourths full. Bake until cooked through, 20 to 25 minutes, or until only moist crumbs cling to a skewer or knife inserted into muffins.

320 ⚡ Poached Pears with Irish Whiskey Sauce

PREP: 45 minutes   COOK: 20 to 30 minutes   CHILL: 5 hours
SERVES: 8 to 10

There is nothing lovelier than a platter of glistening pears on a dessert buffet. Guests who would shun a caloric dessert are delighted with this beautifully presented fruit.

1½ cups sugar
1 lemon, halved
1 vanilla bean, split
2 cloves

10 small firm, ripe pears, such as
   Bosc, or 20 seckel pears, peeled
¼ cup Irish whiskey
Fresh mint sprigs

1. In a large nonreactive flameproof casserole, bring sugar and 6 cups water to a boil over high heat, stirring to dissolve sugar. Reduce heat to low and add lemon, vanilla bean, cloves, and pears. Cook, partially covered, until pears are just barely tender when pierced with a knife, 20 to 30 minutes. Remove from heat and let pears cool in poaching liquid. Refrigerate, covered, in liquid until well chilled, about 4 hours or as long as overnight.

2. Drain pears, reserving liquid. Strain liquid into a saucepan, discarding lemon and cloves and reserving vanilla bean for other use. Boil over high heat until syrup is reduced to 2 cups. Remove from heat and stir in Irish whiskey. Let cool and refrigerate until chilled, about 1 hour.

3. To serve, arrange pears upright on a rimmed serving plate and drizzle with sauce. Using the tip of a sharp knife, insert a small mint sprig near stem of each pear to resemble leaves. Serve cold or at room temperature.

BOXING DAY SUPPER

SERVES: 6

Bubble and Squeak
Potato Croquettes
Carrots in Gravy

Victorian Winter Salad

Mince Pie

BOXING DAY

In England, the day after Christmas is a bank or official holiday. Traditionally the servants had this day off to have their Christmas celebration. The family of the house ate Christmas dinner leftovers, and then went off to visit friends and deliver presents. Start a new tradition by inviting your friends and family over for a Boxing Day Supper.

321 ⟨N⟩ Bubble and Squeak

PREP: 10 minutes   COOK: 30 to 35 minutes   SERVES: 6

Bubble and Squeak is one of those homestyle winter dishes that have been sticking to British ribs for centuries. It's said the dish was named for the sound of the frying meat and cabbage. Back two hundred years ago, this Boxing Day favorite was made with cabbage and slices of cold boiled beef. Most of us today would prefer cooked smoked ham, but sticklers for tradition can use leftover boiled or roast beef.

3 pounds green cabbage
3 tablespoons butter
1¼ pounds fully cooked smoked
   ham, thickly sliced

1 large onion, sliced
½ to 1 teaspoon salt
¼ teaspoon pepper

1. Remove tough outer leaves from cabbage. Core cabbage and slice about ½ inch thick. Bring a large pot of salted water to a boil. Add cabbage and cook until firm-tender, 8 to 10 minutes. Drain cabbage in a colander and let cool. Coarsely chop cabbage.

2. In a large flameproof casserole, melt 1 tablespoon butter over medium heat. Add ham slices and cook, turning, until lightly browned on both sides, 2 to 3 minutes. Remove to a plate.

3. Melt remaining 2 tablespoons butter in same pan over medium heat. Add onion and cook, stirring occasionally, until translucent, 5 to 7 minutes. Add cabbage, stir well, and cook, stirring occasionally, until cabbage and onion are lightly browned, 10 to 12 minutes.

4. Add ham slices to cabbage and onion and cook for 2 to 3 minutes to blend flavors. Season with salt to taste and pepper before serving.

322   Potato Croquettes

PREP: 10 minutes   STAND: 20 minutes   COOK: 35 minutes
SERVES: 6

It's best to start this recipe a few hours before dinnertime because the potato mixture should be cooled and firm before you try to handle it. The croquettes can be prepared an hour or two before frying, which makes them quite manageable for entertaining.

*1½ pounds baking potatoes,
    peeled and cut into 2-inch
    chunks
3 tablespoons butter
3 tablespoons milk
½ teaspoon salt
¼ teaspoon pepper*

*1 medium onion, finely chopped
2 eggs
1 cup flour
1 cup fine dry bread crumbs
Vegetable oil, for deep-frying
1 tablespoon minced parsley
Lemon wedges*

1. In a large saucepan of lightly salted boiling water, cook potatoes until tender, about 20 minutes. Drain and let stand until dry. Rice or mash until smooth. Add 2 tablespoons butter, 2 tablespoons milk, salt, and pepper and mix well. Set aside to cool thoroughly.

2. In a medium skillet, melt remaining 1 tablespoon butter. Add onion and cook over medium heat until translucent, 5 to 7 minutes. Add to cooled mashed potatoes. Lightly beat 1 egg and add to potatoes; mix well. In a small bowl, beat remaining egg with remaining 1 tablespoon milk and set aside.

3. Form potato mixture into 1½-inch balls. Roll in flour, dip in beaten egg, and roll in bread crumbs to coat. Let croquettes dry, preferably on a wire rack, for at least 20 minutes before frying.

4. In a large heavy saucepan or deep-fryer, heat oil to 375°F. Fry croquettes in batches, without crowding, until golden brown, about 5 minutes, turning so croquettes brown evenly. Drain on paper towels. Place on a serving plate and garnish with parsley and lemon wedges.

323 🐿 Carrots in Gravy

PREP: 10 minutes   COOK: 35 minutes   SERVES: 6

3 tablespoons butter
2 pounds carrots, peeled and cut
  ½ inch thick
1 medium onion, chopped
2 tablespoons flour
1 tablespoon minced parsley

1 cup unsalted chicken stock or
  reduced-sodium canned broth
½ teaspoon salt
¼ teaspoon pepper
¼ teaspoon grated nutmeg

1. In a large heavy saucepan, melt butter over low heat. Add carrots, cover and cook, stirring occasionally, until firm-tender, 20 to 25 minutes. With a slotted spoon, remove carrots to a bowl.

2. Add onion to butter remaining in saucepan. Increase heat to medium and cook, stirring occasionally, until lightly browned, about 10 minutes. Sprinkle in flour and cook, stirring constantly, until flour is golden, 3 or 4 minutes. Add parsley and whisk in stock. Bring to a boil, whisking, until gravy is smooth and thick. Season with salt, pepper, and nutmeg.

3. Return carrots to saucepan and reduce heat to low. Cook until carrots are heated through, 1 to 2 minutes. Serve hot.

324 ✒ Victorian Winter Salad

PREP: 10 minutes   COOK: 45 to 55 minutes   SERVES: 6

The winter salad and dressing that follow are adapted from Isabella Beeton's 1861 classic *Book of Household Management*. To add snap to the dish, Beeton called for "mustard-and-cress"— sprouted pepper cress and white mustard seeds. Radish sprouts or watercress will do just fine.

6 medium beets or 1 (16-ounce) can whole beets	⅓ cup heavy cream
4 eggs	⅓ cup tarragon vinegar
1 teaspoon Dijon mustard	4 large Belgian endives
¼ teaspoon white pepper	3 celery ribs
⅛ teaspoon cayenne	1 cup radish sprouts or watercress leaves

1. If using fresh beets, cut off all but 1 to 2 inches of tops and scrub roots in cold water, being careful not to break skin. Place in a medium saucepan and cover with boiling water. Cook, covered, over medium-low heat until beets are tender, 35 to 45 minutes. Drain, let cool completely, and peel. If using canned beets, drain.

2. In a medium saucepan, place eggs in lightly salted cold water over medium-low heat. Bring just barely to a boil and simmer 10 to 12 minutes. Drain eggs and run cold water over them. Let them cool completely. Peel eggs, cut them in half crosswise and carefully remove yolks. Slice white into rings and rounds and set aside.

3. Put egg yolks into a blender or food processor. Add mustard, pepper, cayenne, and cream. Blend for a second, then gradually add vinegar to make a dressing with consistency of heavy cream. Pour into a pretty serving bowl or pitcher.

4. Cut endives crosswise. Thinly slice celery. Combine with sprouts or watercress and toss all together lightly. Put at center of a serving dish. Cut beets into wedges and garnish salad with beet wedges and reserved egg white rings and slices. Serve on individual plates and pass dressing on the side.

325 ⚜ Mince Pie

PREP: 25 minutes   COOK: 55 minutes   SERVES: 8

This is a new, lighter version of the old-fashioned mince pie. It combines meat and sweet fruits and is a splendid way to use up a bit of leftover roast. Traditionally, mince pie was served warm, with the meal, rather than cold as a dessert; this pie is delicious either way.

2 large baking apples, peeled, cored, and chopped
1 cup diced cooked meat (beef, turkey, or goose)
½ cup raisins
½ cup packed brown sugar
2 tablespoons flour
1 teaspoon grated lemon zest
1 teaspoon cinnamon

½ teaspoon ground mace
¼ teaspoon salt
¼ teaspoon pepper
⅓ cup marsala or cream sherry
2 tablespoons brandy
Prepared pastry for a double-crust pie
2 tablespoons butter

1. Preheat oven to 450°F. In a large mixing bowl, combine chopped apples with meat, raisins, brown sugar, flour, lemon zest, cinnamon, mace, salt, and pepper. Add marsala and brandy and mix well.

2. Line a 9-inch pie plate with pastry. Pour in filling. Dot with butter and put on top crust, sealing edges well and cutting several vents to let out steam. Crimp edge decoratively.

3. Bake 10 minutes. Reduce oven temperature to 350° and bake 45 minutes. If you like, you can glaze top crust with a little milk after 35 minutes have passed. Serve warm.

TWELFTH NIGHT DESSERT PARTY

SERVES: 16 TO 22

Champagne Punch Bowl

Amaretto Mousse
Pear Cranberry Crisp
Vanilla ice cream
Caramel Pecan Sauce
Tiny Chocolate Pecan Pies
Chocolate Chip Almond Coffee Cake

326 ☙ Champagne Punch Bowl

PREP: 10 minutes   COOK: none
MAKES: about 22 (4-ounce) servings

In this recipe, you can experiment, if you like, with different fruit-flavored brandies and liqueurs, using, say, cherry-flavored brandy or crème de cassis to replace some or all of the peach-flavored brandy. The recipe doubles easily for large parties.

1 pint strawberries
2 juice oranges
¼ cup triple sec
½ cup peach-flavored brandy

2 (750-ml) bottles champagne, chilled
1 liter seltzer, chilled
Ice

1. Wash and hull strawberries and cut in half. Put berries in a large punch bowl. Slice oranges and add them to bowl. Sprinkle triple sec and brandy over the fruit. Let fruit macerate in liquor 10 to 15 minutes.

2. Add champagne and seltzer and stir gently. Add a large block of ice and ladle into punch cups.

327 🎋 Amaretto Mousse

PREP: 10 minutes   COOK: 5 to 7 minutes   CHILL: 4 hours
SERVES: 8 to 10

Serve a scoop of this rich mousse with a puddle of chocolate sauce and a few almond macaroons, such as Italian amaretti.

½ cup sugar
1 envelope (¼ ounce) unflavored gelatin
6 egg yolks

½ cup amaretto
1 cup heavy cream
4 egg whites
¼ teaspoon cream of tartar

1. In a small bowl, combine sugar and gelatin. In a large heat-proof bowl, combine gelatin mixture with egg yolks and beat until thick and light colored, about 7 minutes. Place bowl over a saucepan of simmering water and cook, stirring constantly, until sugar and gelatin have dissolved, 5 to 7 minutes. Stir in amaretto and cook 1 minute longer. Remove from heat and let cool.

2. In a large bowl, whip cream until stiff peaks form. Fold one-third of cream into cooled gelatin base, then fold in remaining cream.

3. In another large bowl, beat egg whites and cream of tartar until soft peaks form. Fold one-third of egg whites into gelatin base, then fold in remaining egg whites.

4. Cover mousse and refrigerate at least 4 hours or overnight.

NOTE: Because of the threat of salmonella, U.S. Government officials recommend that the very young, the elderly, pregnant women, and people with serious illnesses or weakened immune systems not eat raw or lightly cooked eggs. Keep this in mind and consume raw or lightly cooked eggs at your own risk.

328 🕭 Pear Cranberry Crisp

PREP: 20 minutes   BAKE: 35 to 40 minutes   SERVES: 6 to 8

Whether served with a scoop of frozen vanilla yogurt or topped with a cloud of whipped cream, crisps are a year-round favorite. This recipe elevates winter's humble fruits to a new level of sophistication.

6 cups peeled, cored, and sliced
  pears (3 to 4 large pears)
1½ cups fresh cranberries
¼ cup granulated sugar
¾ cup packed light brown sugar
¾ cup flour
½ teaspoon ground cinnamon

¼ teaspoon salt
1 stick (4 ounces) butter, cut into
  bits
1 cup coarsely chopped walnuts or
  pecans
½ cup rolled oats

1. Preheat oven to 350°F. Combine pears and cranberries in a greased shallow 2-quart baking dish. Sprinkle granulated sugar over fruit.

2. In a large bowl, combine brown sugar, flour, cinnamon, and salt. Stir until well mixed. Cut in butter until mixture resembles coarse meal. Mix in nuts and oats. Sprinkle mixture evenly over fruit.

3. Bake until top is lightly browned and fruit is bubbly, 35 to 40 minutes. Serve warm or at room temperature.

329 🐿 Caramel Pecan Sauce

PREP: 10 minutes   COOK: 15 to 23 minutes   MAKES: 3 cups

This buttery rich sauce turns plain vanilla ice cream into a three-star dessert. It also makes a welcome holiday gift from your kitchen.

1 cup chopped pecans
2 cups packed light brown sugar
1 cup light corn syrup
1 cup heavy cream

1 stick (4 ounces) butter
¼ cup bourbon or Scotch whisky
2 teaspoons vanilla extract

1. Preheat oven to 325°F. Spread pecans on a baking sheet and bake until lightly browned, 5 to 8 minutes. Set aside.

2. In a large heavy saucepan, combine brown sugar, corn syrup, cream, and butter. Bring to a boil over medium heat. Reduce heat to medium-low and cook, stirring, until mixture is reduced to 3 cups, 10 to 15 minutes.

3. Remove from heat and stir in bourbon, vanilla, and toasted pecans. Let cool. If made in advance, cover and refrigerate up to 2 weeks. Serve at room temperature.

330 🌰 Tiny Chocolate Pecan Pies

PREP: 40 minutes   COOK: 25 minutes   MAKES: 36

This dessert is no more than a mouthful, but what a mouthful!

Vegetable cooking spray
Cream Cheese Pastry
  (see page 170)
4 ounces semisweet chocolate, cut
  into ½-inch pieces
1½ cups packed light brown sugar
2 tablespoons butter, softened

2 eggs
1 tablespoon bourbon (optional)
1 teaspoon vanilla extract
Dash salt
1 cup chopped pecans (about
  4 ounces)
36 pecan halves for garnish

1. Preheat oven to 350°F. Oil insides of 36 mini muffin cups with vegetable cooking spray. Press about 2 teaspoons pastry evenly into each muffin cup to line bottom and sides. Refrigerate.

2. In a food processor, chop chocolate into fine bits. Remove from processor and set aside. Add sugar and butter to same bowl and process until well blended. Add eggs, bourbon, if using, vanilla, and salt and process until well blended. Mix in chocolate and chopped pecans. Distribute mixture evenly among pastry shells, filling about three-fourths full. Top each with a pecan half.

3. Bake until pastry is lightly browned and filling is puffed, about 25 minutes. Let cool in tins on a wire rack 30 minutes; then remove pies from cups and let cool completely. Store airtight up to 2 days or freeze.

331 ⚜ Chocolate Chip Almond Coffee Cake

PREP: 10 minutes   COOK: 40 to 45 minutes   SERVES: 12 to 14

1¼ cups sugar
2 tablespoons unsweetened cocoa
   powder
½ teaspoon cinnamon
6 ounces semisweet chocolate chips
   (1 cup)
1 stick (4 ounces) unsalted butter,
   softened
4 ounces almond paste, broken
   into pieces

2 eggs
1½ teaspoons vanilla extract
1½ cups flour
1½ teaspoons baking powder
1 teaspoon baking soda
¼ teaspoon salt
1 cup sour cream

1. Preheat oven to 350°F. Grease and flour a 10-inch tube pan. In a small bowl, combine ¼ cup sugar, cocoa powder, and cinnamon. Stir or whisk gently to mix. Stir in chocolate chips and set aside.

2. In a large bowl, using a hand-held electric mixer, beat butter and remaining 1 cup sugar until light and fluffy. Add almond paste and beat until smooth. Add eggs, one at a time, beating well after each addition. Mix in vanilla.

3. In a medium bowl, combine flour, baking powder, baking soda, and salt. Whisk to mix. Add alternately with sour cream to batter, beginning and ending with dry ingredients.

4. Spoon half of batter into pan. Sprinkle all of cocoa mixture evenly over batter. Top with remaining batter.

5. Bake 40 to 45 minutes, or until a toothpick inserted in center of cake comes out clean. Leave in pan on wire rack 10 minutes. Unmold cake and let cool completely on rack.

Visions of Sugarplums

Sweet traditions exist all over the world and probably have since the beginning of time. As long ago as 2000 B.C., a no-doubt corpulent Egyptian noted, "Cakes were my daily bread." In Germany, cookies in the shape of horses were sacrificed to the gods by those too poor to offer the real thing, and in Scandinavia, honey cakes were thought to appease the god of thunder at the winter solstice. Even today in southern France, before leaving for midnight mass on Christmas Eve, the inhabitants of Provence celebrate the *reveillon* with thirteen desserts representing Christ and his twelve apostles. Americans usually need no excuse, especially during the Christmas season, to indulge their sweet tooth and appease nothing more than their appetite. Christmas is the season of sweet memories. In this chapter a recipe for those enchanting sugarplums that the kids can make leads off an array of unforgettable sweet treats to create for your family, to bring to holiday parties, and to send to faraway friends and relations.

332 🎵 Packing Notice

If you want to send some of these sweets to faraway friends, choose the most sturdy ones, like the Crunchy Peanut Drops or the Apricot and Almond Spice Bars. In general it's not a good idea to mix crisp and chewy cookies together, as the former will go limp as they absorb moisture from the latter. Place the cookies into fluted paper baking cups, then line a decorative airtight tin with gold or silver Mylar wrapping paper. Ship the tin in a cardboard box with padding of newspaper or stale air-popped popcorn (not buttered). Shake the box before taping: If there's any rattling, add more padding.

333 🎵 Sugarplums

PREP: 30 to 35 minutes   COOK: none   MAKES: about 100

Making sugarplums is a perfect holiday project for kids: It takes a bit of time; the work's a trifle sticky; and it requires neither cooking nor sharp utensils. Sugarplums can be stored in an airtight container with wax paper between the layers, or they can be wrapped in aluminum foil, then brightly colored tissue paper.

1 (24-ounce) container pitted prunes
4 ounces whole blanched almonds

1 cup sweetened flaked coconut (4 ounces)
¼ cup sugar

Stuff each prune with an almond, molding fruit around nut into a nice plum shape. In a small bowl, toss coconut and sugar. Roll stuffed prunes in mixture. Store in an airtight container or wrap some or all individually.

334 ✒ Crunchy Peanut Drops

PREP: 10 minutes   BAKE: 10 to 12 minutes   MAKES: about 60

Here's a cookie for the Goober enthusiast—a peanut butter dough filled with chopped roasted peanuts. You can chop the peanuts by hand or pulse them for two or three seconds in a food processor.

1 stick (4 ounces) unsalted butter
½ cup peanut butter
1 cup packed light brown sugar
1 egg
2 tablespoons milk
1 teaspoon vanilla extract

1¼ cups flour
½ teaspoon baking powder
Pinch salt
1 (8-ounce) jar unsalted, dry-roasted peanuts, coarsely chopped (about 1½ cups)

1. Preheat oven to 350°F. In a large mixing bowl, beat together butter, peanut butter, and brown sugar. Beat in egg, milk, and vanilla extract.

2. In a medium bowl, combine flour, baking powder, and salt. Stir or whisk gently to mix well. Add flour mixture to peanut butter mixture by thirds, mixing well after each addition to make a thick, soft dough. Stir in chopped peanuts.

3. Drop dough by heaping teaspoonfuls about 2 inches apart onto ungreased cookie sheets. Bake 10 to 12 minutes, until bottoms of cookies are lightly browned. Let cool on cookie sheets for 3 or 4 minutes, then remove to wire racks and let cool completely.

335 🌾 Lemon Poppyseed Cookies

PREP: 10 minutes   CHILL: 4 hours   BAKE: 12 minutes
MAKES: about 48

Here's an up-to-date flavor combination for the old-fashioned icebox cookie, with all its make-ahead convenience. Wrapped tightly in plastic, the dough will keep in the refrigerator for a week or two, in the freezer for up to two months. It's ready for baking as soon as the dough is soft enough to slice.

1½ sticks (6 ounces) unsalted butter, softened
1 cup sugar
2 tablespoons poppyseeds
2 teaspoons grated lemon zest
2 cups flour
Pinch salt

1. With an electric mixer, beat together butter and sugar until light and fluffy. Mix in poppyseeds and lemon zest. Add flour and salt and mix well to make a stiff dough.

2. Divide dough in half and roll each piece in wax paper to make a cylinder about 2 inches in diameter and 6 inches long. Refrigerate dough until firm, at least 4 hours.

3. Preheat oven to 350°F. Grease cookie sheets. Slice dough into rounds about ¼ inch thick. Arrange about 1 inch apart on cookie sheets. Bake 12 minutes, or until edges of cookies are lightly browned. Let cookies cool on baking sheet for a few seconds, then remove to a wire rack and let cool completely.

336 🌱 Peanut Butter Thumbprints

PREP: 15 minutes   CHILL: 2 hours   BAKE: 13 to 15 minutes
MAKES: about 60

A demitasse spoon or a half-teaspoon measure is ideal for spooning the jam into the thumbprints made in the dough.

*1 stick (4 ounces) unsalted butter,   1 egg
    softened   2 tablespoons milk
½ cup peanut butter   2 cups flour
1¼ cups sugar   ⅔ cup raspberry jam*

1. With an electric mixer, beat together butter and peanut butter until blended. Beat in sugar until mixture is fluffy, then beat in egg and milk. With a spoon, stir in flour to make a thick dough. Gather dough into a ball and put in a bowl just large enough to hold it. Cover bowl and refrigerate at least 2 hours, until well chilled.

2. Preheat oven to 350°F. Butter cookie sheets. Scoop up dough by heaping teaspoonfuls and roll into 1-inch balls. Place balls 2 inches apart on cookie sheets. Gently flatten balls with the palm of your hand and make a little indentation in each with tip of thumb. Spoon ½ teaspoon jam into each indentation.

3. Bake 13 to 15 minutes, until edges of cookies are lightly browned. Let cookies cool on baking sheets 2 to 3 minutes, then remove to wire racks and let cool completely.

337 ❧ Nutty Thumbprints

PREP: 15 minutes   BAKE: 15 to 20 minutes   MAKES: 60 to 72

2⅓ sticks (about 9 ounces) butter,
    softened
⅔ cup sugar
4 eggs, separated
2 teaspoons almond extract
3 cups flour

½ teaspoon salt
1½ cups chopped walnuts or
    pecans (6 ounces)
1 cup seedless raspberry jam or
    jelly

1. Preheat oven to 350°F. In a medium bowl, beat butter and sugar until light and fluffy. Mix in egg yolks, one at a time, until well blended. Beat in almond extract.

2. Sift flour and salt together and gradually mix into butter mixture. Shape rounded tablespoons of dough into small balls.

3. Beat egg whites lightly with a fork. Set nuts on a plate or sheet of wax paper. Dip each ball of dough into egg whites, then in chopped nuts to coat. Set 1 inch apart on ungreased cookie sheets. Press your thumb gently into center of each ball.

4. Bake until cookies are lightly browned, 15 to 20 minutes. Transfer to a rack and let cool.

5. Fill center of each cookie with scant teaspoon jam or jelly. Store airtight up to 3 days or freeze.

338 ❧ Fresh Ginger Cookies

PREP: 5 minutes   CHILL: 1 hour   BAKE: 8 to 10 minutes
MAKES: about 60

1½ sticks (6 ounces) butter,
    softened
1 cup sugar
1 cup unsulphured molasses
2 eggs

4½ cups flour
2 tablespoons grated fresh ginger
2 teaspoons baking soda
1½ teaspoons cinnamon
1 teaspoon salt

1. In a large bowl, beat together butter and sugar until light and fluffy. Blend in molasses. Add eggs one at a time, beating well after each addition. Add flour, ginger, baking soda, cinnamon, and salt, stirring until well combined. Cover and refrigerate 1 hour.

2. Preheat oven to 400°F. Grease cookie sheets. Roll dough into 1½-inch balls and place 1 inch apart on cookie sheets. Flatten balls slightly with bottom of a glass or palm of your hand.

3. Bake 8 to 10 minutes. Remove to racks and let cool.

339 🐿 Moravian Spice Cookies

PREP: 10 minutes   CHILL: 1 hour   BAKE: 8 minutes
MAKES: about 72

1 cup packed dark brown sugar
2 cups molasses
1 stick (4 ounces) unsalted butter,
  melted
½ cup vegetable oil

4 cups flour
1½ teaspoons baking soda
1 tablespoon cinnamon
2 teaspoons ground cloves
2 teaspoons ground ginger

1. In a large bowl, using a hand-held electric mixer, beat sugar, molasses, butter, and oil until light and fluffy.

2. Add 2 cups flour, baking soda, cinnamon, cloves, and ginger and mix well. Continue adding flour, ½ cup at a time, mixing until just incorporated; dough will be stiff. Divide dough in half. Flatten into disks and wrap with plastic wrap. Refrigerate 1 hour or longer.

3. Preheat oven to 350°F. On a lightly floured board or between 2 sheets of wax paper, roll out half of dough. Cut with a 2-inch cookie cutter or glass rim and place on cookie sheet. Bake until lightly brown, 8 minutes. Remove cookies from pan and cool on wire rack.

340 ✿ Linzer Squares with Streusel Topping

PREP: 20 minutes   BAKE: 35 to 40 minutes   MAKES: 9

These buttery raspberry squares are perfect little gems to serve at a holiday dessert reception.

1½ cups flour
¼ teaspoon salt
1¼ cups ground almonds (about 5 ounces)
1½ sticks (6 ounces) unsalted butter, softened
1 cup powdered sugar

2 egg yolks
1 teaspoon vanilla extract
½ teaspoon almond extract
1 (12-ounce) jar seedless red raspberry preserves
1 tablespoon lemon juice

1. Preheat oven to 350°F. Lightly grease a 9-inch square baking pan. In a medium bowl, combine flour, salt, and 1 cup almonds. Mix lightly.

2. In another medium bowl, using a hand-held electric mixer, mix butter and ¾ cup powdered sugar until light and fluffy. Add egg yolks, vanilla, and almond extract and beat until well combined. Add flour mixture and stir until just blended.

3. Press two-thirds of dough onto bottom of pan. In a small bowl, stir together preserves and lemon juice. Spread preserves evenly over dough.

4. With 2 knives or a pastry blender, cut remaining ¼ cup almonds into remaining dough. Mixture will be crumbly. Scatter over preserves. Bake until golden brown, 35 to 40 minutes. Let cool in pan on wire rack. Sprinkle remaining ¼ cup powdered sugar over top. Cut into 9 squares.

341 🐦 Pumpkin Pecan Apple Cake

PREP: 5 minutes   BAKE: 45 to 50 minutes   SERVES: 9

¾ cup pecans (3 ounces)
1½ sticks (6 ounces) unsalted butter, softened
1¼ cups packed brown sugar
3 eggs
1 cup canned pumpkin puree
2 medium Delicious apples, peeled, cored, and shredded

2 cups flour
2 teaspoons baking powder
1 teaspoon baking soda
1 teaspoon cinnamon
½ teaspoon grated nutmeg
¼ teaspoon ground ginger
¼ teaspoon salt

1. Preheat oven to 350°F. Grease and flour a 9-inch square baking pan. Place pecans in a small baking dish and toast in oven until very lightly browned and fragrant, about 5 minutes. Leave oven on. Coarsely chop nuts.

2. In a large bowl, using a hand-held electric mixer, beat butter and brown sugar until light and fluffy. Add eggs, one at a time, beating well after each addition. Mix in pumpkin puree and apples.

3. Add flour, baking powder, baking soda, cinnamon, nutmeg, ginger, and salt. Mix until just blended. Stir in toasted pecans.

4. Spread into pan. Bake until top is golden and toothpick inserted in center comes out clean, 45 to 50 minutes. Let set in pan 10 minutes, then remove to wire rack to cool. Cut into 9 squares before serving.

342 🐦 Apple Raspberry Tart

PREP: 20 minutes   BAKE: 35 to 40 minutes   SERVES: 8 to 10

This no-fuss tart looks like a fruit pizza. It's as much fun to eat with your hands, cut into wedges, as it is on a plate as the finish to an elegant meal.

1 cup flour
2 tablespoons ground walnuts
¼ teaspoon salt
5 tablespoons cold butter
2 to 3 tablespoons cold water
4 to 5 large baking apples, peeled
   and thinly sliced (4 cups)

¼ cup sugar
2 tablespoons flour
¼ teaspoon cinnamon
¼ cup fresh or frozen raspberries

1. In a medium bowl, stir together flour, walnuts, and salt. Grate cold butter into flour mixture by using the largest holes on a box grater, stirring the butter in as you grate, so it will not stick together. Stir in cold water little by little, adding enough to just bring the dough together. Form into a ball and refrigerate while making filling.

2. In a large bowl, stir together apples, sugar, flour, cinnamon, and raspberries.

3. Preheat oven to 350°F. Shape dough into a flat circle and roll out to 10 to 11 inches in diameter. Set pastry on a baking sheet. Place filling in center of dough and spread out to cover, leaving a 1½-inch margin all around. Bring dough up to overlap edge of filling all around tart.

4. Bake 35 to 40 minutes, or until crust is golden brown and filling is bubbling. Let cool before serving.

343 🕊 Apricot and Almond Spice Bars

PREP: 10 minutes   BAKE: 40 to 45 minutes   MAKES: 30

1½ sticks (6 ounces) butter,
   softened
½ cup packed light brown sugar
1 egg
1 teaspoon vanilla extract
1 cup flour
¼ teaspoon salt

1 cup finely ground almonds
   (about 4 ounces)
¼ teaspoon cinnamon
¼ teaspoon ground allspice
½ teaspoon grated lemon zest
⅔ cup apricot preserves

1. Preheat oven to 350°F. Grease a 9- x 13-inch baking pan. In a medium bowl, beat together butter and sugar. Add egg and vanilla and beat well. Add flour, salt, almonds, cinnamon, allspice, and lemon zest and mix until blended.

2. Pat half of the dough into pan. Spread apricot preserves over dough. With floured hands, pat pieces of dough thin in your hands and place on top of preserves to form another layer of dough. Do not worry if it isn't completely even or touching in places; dough will spread as it bakes.

3. Bake 40 to 45 minutes, or until medium brown. Cut into 30 rectangles while hot and let cool on a rack.

344 ❦ Eggnog Crème Brûlée

PREP: 15 minutes   BAKE: 48 to 55 minutes
CHILL: 6 hours and 2 hours   SERVES: 8 to 10

This rich classic custard incorporates all the rich flavors of eggnog.

4 cups heavy cream	1 tablespoon vanilla extract
¼ cup granulated sugar	¼ teaspoon grated nutmeg
8 egg yolks	Dash salt
2 tablespoons brandy	1¾ cups packed light brown sugar

1. Position rack in center of oven and preheat to 325°F. In a medium saucepan, combine cream and granulated sugar. Cook over medium heat, stirring, until sugar dissolves and mixture just reaches a boil, 3 to 5 minutes. Remove from heat.

2. In a large mixing bowl, beat egg yolks until light and lemon colored, about 5 minutes. Carefully mix in hot cream, brandy, vanilla, nutmeg, and salt until well blended. Pour mixture through a sieve into a well-greased 2-quart shallow nonreactive baking dish and place in a larger baking pan. Pour enough boiling water into baking pan to reach halfway up sides of dish.

3. Bake until custard is just set around the edges yet still soft in center, 45 to 50 minutes. Remove from water bath and let cool. Cover and refrigerate at least 6 hours or overnight.

4. Preheat broiler. Push brown sugar through a sieve, sprinkling evenly over chilled custard and pressing gently into place. Broil 6 to 8 inches from heat, turning dish as necessary to avoid burning, until sugar melts and begins to caramelize evenly, 3 to 5 minutes. Cover and refrigerate at least 2 hours or as long as 4 hours before serving.

345 ✒ Cranberry Bread Pudding

PREP: 15 minutes   BAKE: 1 hour 10 minutes   SERVES: 8 to 10

This eggnog-scented dessert dotted with dried cranberries is warm and comforting any time of day. Dried cranberries are often sold loose in the produce section of many supermarkets or packaged as "ruby raisins."

¾ cup dried cranberries
1 (1-pound) loaf egg bread, torn
  into 1½-inch pieces (about
  12 cups)
6 tablespoons butter, melted

4 eggs
1 cup sugar
4 cups milk
2½ teaspoons vanilla extract
⅛ teaspoon grated nutmeg

1. Preheat oven to 325°F. Grease a 1½-quart baking dish. In a small heatproof bowl, cover dried cranberries with boiling water and let stand 5 minutes; drain.

2. In baking dish, toss bread with melted butter until well coated.

3. In a large bowl, combine eggs and sugar. Beat until well mixed. Stir in milk, vanilla, and nutmeg until well blended. Pour mixture over bread, cover with foil, and bake 40 minutes. Uncover and bake 30 minutes longer, or until a knife inserted into center of custard comes out clean. Serve warm, at room temperature, or chilled.

346 🌰 Ginger Shortbread

PREP: 15 minutes   BAKE: 1 hour   MAKES: 12 to 16

Ginger gives this moist and buttery shortbread a spicy fillip. Best of all, the flavor actually improves with age.

2 cups flour
1 cup packed light brown sugar
1 tablespoon ground ginger

Dash of salt
2 sticks (8 ounces) butter, softened

1. Preheat oven to 325°F. In a food processor, combine flour, brown sugar, ginger, and salt. Mix briefly until well blended. Add butter and process until mixture resembles coarse meal; do not overprocess. Turn out dough.

2. Pat dough evenly over bottom of an ungreased 9-inch tart pan or springform with a removable bottom. Press tines of a fork around edge to form a decorative border. Pierce dough every 2 inches with fork.

3. Bake 1 hour, or until lightly browned and center is firm. Remove sides of pan and score into thin wedges while still warm. Let cool to room temperature in pan before cutting and serving. Store airtight up to 5 days; freeze for longer storage.

347 🍒 Cranberry Clafouti

PREP: 15 minutes   BAKE: 50 minutes   SERVES: 6

A clafouti is a custardlike pancake studded with fruit. Cranberries give this traditional French country-style dessert a New World twist.

3 eggs	1 teaspoon vanilla extract
⅔ cup flour	Dash salt
½ cup sugar	2 cups fresh cranberries
½ cup milk	Grated zest of 1 orange
½ cup heavy cream	Powdered sugar
1 tablespoon bourbon or brandy	

   1. Preheat oven to 350°F. Generously grease a 9-inch glass pie plate or ceramic quiche dish.
   2. Using an electric mixer, blender, or whisk, combine eggs with flour, sugar, milk, cream, bourbon, vanilla, and salt. Mix until well blended. Spread cranberries and orange zest evenly over bottom of pie plate. Carefully pour batter over fruit.
   3. Bake until custard has just set in the center, about 50 minutes. Let cool to lukewarm, sprinkle liberally with powdered sugar, and cut into wedges. Serve warm.

348 ⟨ Chocolate Amaretto Cake

PREP: 30 minutes   BAKE: 40 to 45 minutes   SERVES: 8 to 10

This dense and chocolatey cake is actually better if made a day in advance. If a topping is desired, try the Creamy Amaretto Sauce, a recipe for which follows.

½ pound semisweet chocolate, cut into ½-inch pieces
2 sticks (8 ounces) butter, softened
1 cup sugar
5 eggs, separated
3 tablespoons amaretto

¼ teaspoon almond extract
½ cup flour
⅓ cup crushed almond macaroons, such as Italian amaretti
⅛ teaspoon cream of tartar
Dash salt

1. Preheat oven to 350°F. Generously grease a 9-inch cake pan. Melt chocolate in a small heatproof bowl set over a pan of simmering water. Let cool 5 minutes.

2. Meanwhile, using an electric mixer set at medium speed, beat butter until creamy; mix in sugar. With machine on, add egg yolks, one at a time, until well blended. Add amaretto and almond extract and continue beating until mixture is light and fluffy, about 5 minutes.

3. In a small bowl, combine flour and crushed amaretti. Gradually add to butter mixture, beating until well blended. Mix in melted chocolate.

4. In a large bowl, beat egg whites with cream of tartar and salt until firm, glossy peaks form. Fold one-third of egg whites into chocolate mixture until well blended, then fold in remaining egg whites.

5. Pour batter into prepared pan and bake 40 to 45 minutes, until top of cake appears dry and a tester inserted in center of cake shows only moist crumb. Unmold onto a rack and let cool.

349 🌰 Creamy Amaretto Sauce

PREP: 5 minutes   COOK: none   MAKES: about 1 cup

A quickly made sauce that will make you think twice before ever again topping a dessert with whipped cream. Instead of the almond-based amaretto, you can use other liqueurs for other flavors, Grand Marnier for orange, for example, or simply bourbon.

1 cup sour cream
2½ tablespoons powdered sugar

2 tablespoons amaretto or other liqueur

In a small bowl, combine sour cream, powdered sugar, and amaretto. Stir until well blended. If made in advance, cover and refrigerate up to 1 week.

350 🐦 Chocolate Indiscretions

PREP: 15 minutes   BAKE: 15 minutes   CHILL: 2 hours
MAKES: 20

These chewy little chocolate cakes are not quite a sin, merely an indiscretion. Dust with powdered sugar and serve like a cupcake. Or remove the foil, invert onto a serving plate, and top with a dab of whipped cream or Creamy Amaretto Sauce (preceding recipe).

1 pound semisweet chocolate, broken into ½-inch pieces
1½ sticks (6 ounces) butter, cut into bits
6 eggs
1 tablespoon sugar
½ cup amaretto or other liqueur
1 teaspoon vanilla extract
¼ cup flour

1. Preheat oven to 350°F. Place 20 foil baking cups on a baking sheet. Melt chocolate and butter in a double boiler or in a medium heatproof bowl set over a pan of simmering water, stirring until smooth and well blended. Let cool 10 minutes.

2. Using an electric mixer, beat eggs at medium speed until light and fluffy, about 5 minutes. Beat in sugar, amaretto, vanilla, and flour until well blended.

3. Fold one-third of egg mixture into melted chocolate until well blended, then fold in remaining egg mixture. Using a ⅓-cup measure, fill baking cups three-fourths full.

4. Bake 15 minutes, or until tops are barely dry and slightly cracked and centers look underdone. Let cool. Freeze at least 2 hours or refrigerate to set. Store frozen and thaw 1 hour before serving.

PART SIX

Looking Back & Ahead

CHAPTER 11

Tried & True & New Traditions

Everything about Christmas is tradition—the
tree, Santa Claus, stockings, cards. These
traditions are already in place; they are the
framework within which each family weaves
its own cherished customs. Family traditions
link the face of the bright-eyed child at the
table to the fading portrait over the mantel,
the new country to the old, the new century
to the old century. Rituals may differ from
region to region, from family to family, but
they are only variations on a theme. For
despite the persistent commercialization of
Christmas, the beauty and joy of its simple
message of peace on earth and goodwill
to men remains.

351 🎄 The Yule Log: Traditional & Edible

The yule log had its origins in an ancient pagan festival in celebration of the winter solstice. A huge fire was kindled to light and warm the shortest day of the year. A large log was used as a foundation for the fire, which was kindled by a log from the last year's fire. The tradition endured, and you find it even today in rural areas of France. If you have a fireplace, start this age-old tradition in your home. Carefully pick one log from the fire, allow it to cool completely, and then store it in the cellar or yard until next year.

If you don't have a fireplace and want to have a yule log, make a Bûche de Noël and tell your guests how this tradition got started (see page 204).

THE GINGERBREAD HOUSE

Gingerbread dates back to olden times, but the colorfully decorated gingerbread house so popular at Christmas comes from Jakob Grimm's fairy tale, *Hansel and Gretel*. Lost in the enchanted forest, Hansel and Gretel nibbled at the witch's tasty gingerbread house. Bake your own gingerbread cottage alone with your children or have them invite their friends over for an afternoon of baking and decorating. It may turn into something you do every year.

352 🎄 Gingerbread Cottage

Here's a chance to build your dream house for only a few dollars. This is a labor of love, but the end result will delight all. Like any good architect, you must begin with blueprints; in this case, they are templates cut from heavy paper. You will need:

1 template, 8½ X 4 inches, to
  make 2 side walls
1 template, 9 X 4½ inches, to
  make 2 roof pieces
1 peaked template to make 2 end
  walls: 5¼ inches wide and
  4 inches tall, with a 4-inch-
  tall peak extending from each
  side; from peak to foundation,
  this piece is 7 inches tall

Gingerbread (recipe follows)
Royal Mortar (see page 250)
1 piece wood or heavy cardboard
  at least 10 X 13 inches, for the
  foundation
1 piece heavy paper or light
  cardboard, 9 X 9 inches, to
  reinforce roof
Assorted candies, to decorate
  cottage

1. To make the cottage, prepare the gingerbread and use templates to cut out walls. Bake and cool thoroughly. When you are ready to build, prepare a batch of royal mortar.

2. Place wood or cardboard foundation on a table. Spread a thick layer of royal mortar where you want to start building. Cover edges of 1 side and 1 end of gingerbread walls with mortar. Place walls into mortar on foundation and carefully press corners together at a right angle. As soon as walls can stand up independently, strengthen inside seam of walls with mortar. Let dry 15 minutes. (You may wish to use long straight pins to reinforce the joints; do not press them all the way in if you intend to eat the cottage. Keep track of how many you use, so you can count when removing them.)

3. Repeat process with remaining side and end walls, attaching them also to other two walls. Coat all edges with mortar, including inside seams. Let dry 15 minutes or longer.

5. Fold roof reinforcement cardboard in half. Unfold and use mortar to glue the 2 gingerbread roof pieces to cardboard, with crease in center. Let dry 15 minutes or longer.

6. Generously coat top edges of all walls with mortar. Carefully lift roof piece, bending in center to create a ridge. Spread more mortar on part of cardboard that will connect with walls. Place roof on top of cottage, making sure it is centered and juts out evenly on both ends and sides. Let dry thoroughly, at least 1 hour. If there is any mortar remaining, cover with a damp towel. Otherwise, make a new batch to decorate cottage.

353 🎋 Gingerbread

PREP: 25 minutes BAKE: 12 to 18 minutes   CHILL: 1 hour
MAKES: 1 cottage or about 12 (4-inch) gingerbread girls
and boys

1⅓ cups dark molasses
¾ cup sugar
3 tablespoons butter
4 cups flour
2 teaspoons cinnamon

1 teaspoon ground ginger
1 teaspoon baking powder
½ teaspoon baking soda
⅛ teaspoon ground cloves
⅛ teaspoon salt

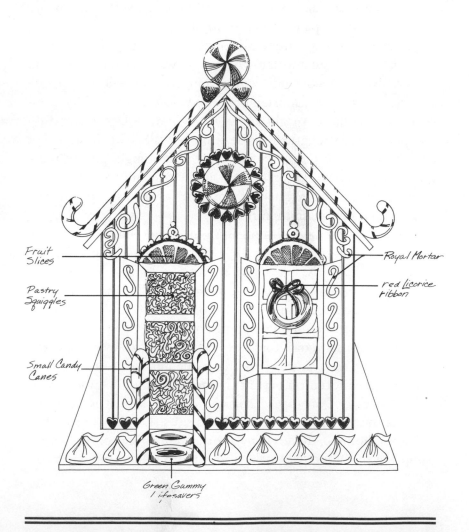

Fruit Slices

Pastry Squiggles

Small Candy Canes

Royal Mortar

red licorice ribbon

Green Gummy Lifesavers

1. In a small saucepan, stir molasses and sugar over low heat until sugar dissolves, 2 to 3 minutes. Mix in butter until melted. Remove from heat.

2. In a large bowl, sift together 2 cups of flour, with cinnamon, ginger, baking powder, baking soda, cloves, and salt. Stir in molasses mixture until well blended. Gradually stir in remaining flour until mixture forms a sticky dough.

3. Divide dough in half and pat out evenly on 2 parchment-lined cookie sheets (15½- x 10¼-inch size). Cover surface with plastic wrap and use a rolling pin to even the dough to about 3/8 inch thick. Refrigerate until thoroughly chilled, 1 hour or as long as 3 days.

4. Preheat oven to 350°F. Remove plastic from dough and cut walls and roofs for a gingerbread cottage, using templates. Or make gingerbread people or other shapes using a cookie cutter. Carefully remove excess dough from baking sheets. (Excess dough can be used for cookies or to create decorations for your cottage, like trees or fences.)

5. Bake until gingerbread is firm but not browned, 10 to 15 minutes. Carefully transfer to racks and let cool thoroughly.

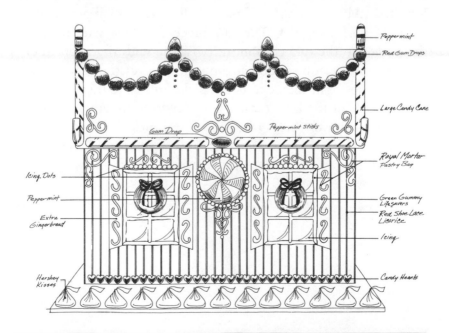

Royal Mortar

PREP: 5 minutes   COOK: none   MAKES: 4 cups

2 egg whites
3½ cups powdered sugar
2 tablespoons lemon juice

Blue food coloring, to prevent
mortar from turning gray

1. In a large bowl with an electric mixer, beat egg whites
until stiff but not dry, 2 to 3 minutes.
2. With beaters running, gradually sift sugar into whites until
well mixed. Beat in lemon juice and 1 very small drop food coloring until mixture is of spreading consistency.

354 🐿 Kissing Ball

The golden bough, thought to be mistletoe, was sacred to the
Romans. Nowadays when mistletoe is hung as a Christmas decoration, it is an invitation for a man to kiss a woman. In the
mid–1700s in America, traditional kissing balls of boxwood and
holly were hung in the windows, suspended from the top by a
long red ribbon. To make a kissing ball, take a small potato, and
pierce it with a skewer. Thread a piece of florist wire through
the potato so the two ends meet; twist the ends together. Insert
six-inch pieces of boxwood all around to cover the entire spud.
Attach sprigs of mistletoe to florist picks and poke them into the
bottom half of the ball. Attach six-inch-long streamers of half-
inch-wide satin or velvet ribbon to floral picks and insert these
as well. Top with a festive rosette bow tied around the florist
wire and hang from a chandelier or over a tall doorway.

355 ✿ Advent Wreath

Advent, meaning the approach or coming, refers to the four Sundays preceding Christmas. Advent is celebrated in church, and in many homes as well. Some people keep an Advent wreath with candles; one is lit on each of the Sundays in Advent to mark the approach of Christmas. Use a store-bought or homemade evergreen wreath (white fir and Colorado spruce hold their needles best) and embellish it with dried flowers. Place four large red candles in it, and in the middle a white candle. Light a red candle on each of the Sundays of Advent and the white one on Christmas Day. Some families use the occasion of the lighting of the candles to add figures to the crèche. Then on Christmas Day, the youngest in the family gets to place the Christ Child in the manger.

NEW TRADITIONS

The nicest thing about traditions is they can be added to any time.

356 ✿ A Quiet Time

Sometimes the holidays are so harried they become a blur. That's why it's important to carve out some quiet moments during the season. Gather the family together and read aloud from one of the following stories, each with a simple message of love at Christmas: Dylan Thomas's "A Child's Christmas in Wales," Truman Capote's "A Christmas Memory," O. Henry's "The Gift of the Magi."

357 ❦ More Special Moments

- Make it a tradition to take the youngsters in the family to see a performance of "The Nutcracker Suite." Their delight will be your gift in return.
- During Christmas week dress the kids in their warmest pjs and pack them, with their blankets, into the car. Then take a leisurely late-night drive through town or city to view the Christmas decorations when there's no one else around.
- Start a collection of Christmas books that runs the gamut from Dickens to *Frosty the Snowman*. Look for them at garage sales, antique shops, and secondhand book shops. Read the stories to the children at bedtime during the Christmas season.
- Take a Christmas photo of the whole family each year, being sure to include the family pets, then start an album of these photos to treasure through the years. To include everyone in the picture, use a camera with a self-timer.

358 ❦ Make a Piñata

In Mexico the highlight of the carnival-like celebration of the birth of Christ is the breaking of the piñata, a papier-mâché or earthenware animal or sphere that is gaily painted and decorated with colored paper and filled with candy, charms, and other small presents. It is hung from the ceiling. Children are blindfolded, twirled around three times, and are given three tries to break open the piñata with a long stick or broom handle.

Round balloon
Petroleum jelly
1 terra-cotta flowerpot
1 cup flour
Sunday comics

Acrylic paint
Colored tissue paper
Elmer's glue
Ribbon 2 inches wide for
   streamers

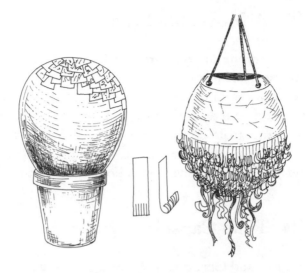

1. Blow up the balloon, tie it off, and rub a thin coat of petroleum jelly on the surface. Balance the balloon in the flowerpot with the tied end down. Put flour in a bowl and add water slowly to make a paste, mixing until it's the consistency of pancake batter.

2. Tear the newspaper into 2-inch-square scraps. Dip individual pieces of paper into the paste, wetting them completely, and apply them to the balloon, overlapping the pieces. Repeat until the entire balloon is covered (except the small area sitting in the flowerpot), then apply 2 more layers of newspaper. Let the papier-mâché dry completely, at least 24 hours. To speed up the process, put the form in a warm oven with the heat turned off.

3. When dry, pop the balloon, remove it, and wipe away any petroleum jelly that sticks to the papier-mâché. Dry for 24 hours more.

4. Paint the piñata with 2 coats of acrylic paint. Cut 6- x 1½-inch strips of tissue paper, cut a 1-inch fringe into 1 end, and curl the fringe carefully with scissors. Working up from the closed end of the piñata, glue on the tissue paper strips, overlapping them. Glue streamers of ribbon and curled tissue paper to the bottom of the piñata.

5. Make 3 holes around the rim of the piñata with an awl and put strings through the holes. Fill with candy and small favors and hang from the ceiling.

359   A Moveable Feast

Instead of everyone in your circle of friends hosting a separate holiday party, make plans to have a progressive dinner. The dinner party moves from one house to another, starting with cocktails and hors d'oeuvres at the first stop, appetizer and/or soup at the second stop, main course at the next, and dessert and coffee at the last. It's an enjoyable way to share the burden, and the glory, and you get to see everyone's holiday decorations too.

360   Time Capsule

Christmas Eve and Christmas Day are the time when the family gathers together. It's a time when memories are made. Capture those memories by creating a family time capsule to be opened in not less than five years. It need not be buried any deeper than the basement, garage, attic, or cluttered hall closet. Take a mailing tube and put in the front page of that day's newspaper, a list of who was present or, better yet, Polaroid photos of everyone. Ask each guest in advance to write down a wish, either for themselves, someone else, or the planet, and a prediction. Other items to include: an audio tape of someone telling a family anecdote, a piece of jewelry to be given a child who in five years will be old enough to wear it, a treasured recipe of grandma's (never before written down), drawings or poems by the children, and some fashion accessory that is already "out" but may be back "in" in five years.

Christmas Past:
A Christmas Diary

The days leading up to Christmas are
impatient days, but when the big day finally
dawns, it's gifts and hugs and laughter galore.
For many, Christmas is the best night and day
of any in the year. When they are finally over,
there's a wonderful exhaustion, a kind of
lovely letdown, softened by the knowledge
that it will all come again next year.

361   It's Never Too Early

The day after Christmas the post-holiday sale season starts. This is the only time it makes sense to buy wrapping paper, ribbon, even cards, all at fifty percent or more off. It is also a good time to buy ornaments and other decorative seasonal items. It's the best time to buy some generic presents for next year. See pages 8 and 9 for what else is on sale in December and January.

362   Try to Remember

The time between Christmas and New Year's is a relatively quiet catch-your-breath period. While the memories of this Christmas are still fresh make your lists: who gave what to whom to avoid duplications (and note which ones were a hit and those that missed), of returns if any to avoid embarrassment, of all the people to whom you sent a card and from whom you received one with updated addresses to make the sending easier next year, of parties you attended, as well as a record of the one/s you gave with guest list and menu.

363 ❧ Additions to Christmas Card List

NAME _____

ADDRESS_____

NAME _____

ADDRESS_____

NAME _____

ADDRESS_____

NAME _____

ADDRESS_____

NAME _____

ADDRESS_____

NAME _____

ADDRESS_____

NAME _____

ADDRESS_____

NAME _____

ADDRESS_____

NAME _____

ADDRESS_____

NAME _____

ADDRESS_____

NAME _____

ADDRESS_____

NAME _____

ADDRESS_____

364 🖋 Gift Lists

GIVEN TO: RECEIVED FROM:

365   My/Our Christmas Party List

DATE: _____   PLACE: _____

GUEST LIST: MENU:

_____   _____

_____   _____

_____   _____

_____   _____

_____   _____

_____   _____

_____   _____

_____   _____

_____   _____

_____   DECORATIONS:

_____   _____

_____   _____

_____   _____

_____   FAVOR:

_____   _____

_____   _____

APPENDIX

TEMPLATES FOR DESIGNS

137   Yummy Tags

137   Yummy Tags

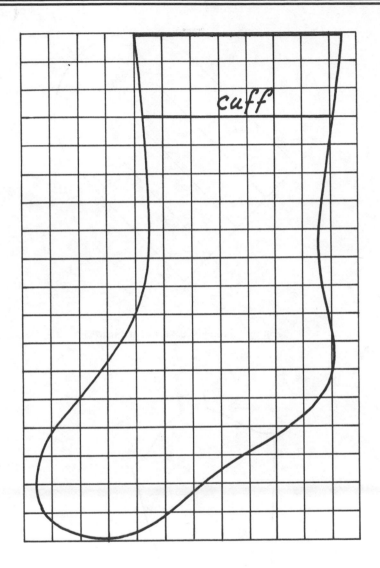

197   A Glimpse of Stockings

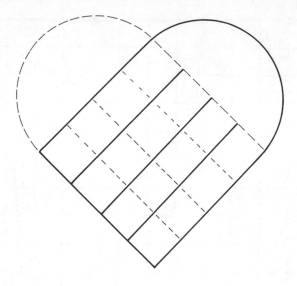

234   Basket Weave Paper Hearts

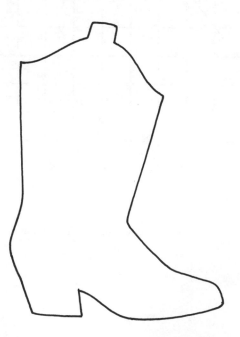

244   Boot Pattern

239   Paper Cutout Chains

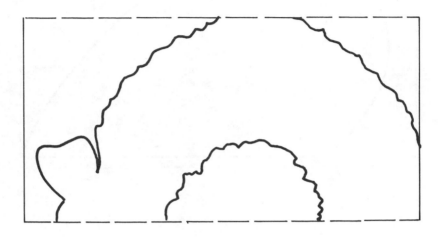

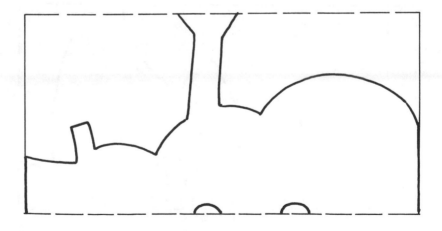

239   Paper Cutout Chains

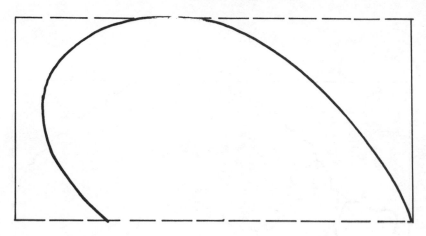

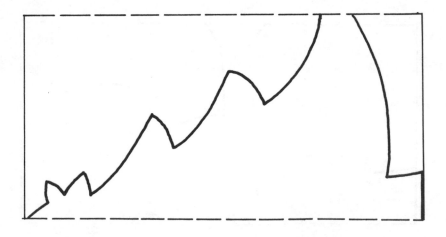

INDEX

ACKNOWLEDGMENTS

I would like to thank the following people for their endless help and encouragement: Marilyn Buckland, Mardoe Cavalero, Daria Enrick, Beth Flusser, Jay McElynn, Phillip Manin, Jennifer Moyer, Ruth Sager, and Irene Tanczy.

I owe a particular debt of gratitude to Marilyn Appleberg for her dedication, organization, and countless hours of work which brought this book to life.

ABOUT THE AUTHORS

David E. Monn is the president of David E. Monn Interior Design, Inc., a New York City–based design and decoration firm. An entertaining entrepreneur, he has arranged everything from intimate teas for two to sit-down dinners for four hundred.

Marilyn J. Appleberg is the author of the *I Love ...* travel guides to major American cities. In addition to loving New York, Washington, D.C., Boston, Chicago, San Francisco, and Los Angeles, she is simply mad about Christmas.

To order any of the
365 Ways Cookbooks

visit your local bookseller or call 1-800-321-6890

Our bestselling **365 Ways Cookbooks** are wire-bound to lie flat and have colorful, wipe-clean Kivar® covers.

Each **365 Ways Cookbook** is $16.95 plus $3.50 per copy shipping and handling. Applicable sales tax will be billed to your account. No CODs. Please allow 4–6 weeks for delivery.

> **Please have your Visa, MasterCard, or American Express card at hand when calling.**

◆ 365 ◆

Easy Italian Recipes 0-06-016310-0

Easy Low-Calorie Recipes 0-06-016309-7

Easy One-Dish Meals 0-06-016311-9

Great Barbecue & Grilling Recipes 0-06-016224-4

Great Chocolate Desserts 0-06-016537-5

Great Cookies and Brownies 0-06-016840-4

Quick & Easy Microwave Recipes 0-06-016026-8

Snacks, Hors D'Oeuvres & Appetizers 0-06-016536-7

Ways to Cook Chicken 0-06-015539-6

Ways to Cook Fish and Shellfish 0-06-016841-2

Ways to Cook Hamburger & Other Ground Meats
0-06-016535-9

Ways to Cook Pasta 0-06-015865-4

Ways to Prepare for Christmas 0-06-017048-4

Ways to Wok 0-06-016643-6

FORTHCOMING TITLES

Easy Chinese Recipes 0-06-016961-3

Great Dessert Recipes 0-06-016959-1

Meatless Recipes 0-06-016958-3

Mexican Recipes 0-06-016963-X

20-Minute Menus 0-06-016962-1

Soups and Stews 0-06-016960-5

Also available in wire-bound format are:

The Bartender's Bible 0-06-016722-X $12.95
The Best Bread Machine Cookbook Ever 0-06-016927-3
$15.95

X02011